Antique Furniture

A BASIC PRIMER ON FURNITURE
FEATURING 25 DISTINCT PERIODS

COLLECTOR BOOKS

A Division of Schroeder Publishing Co., Inc.

CONTENTS

INTRODUCTION

In 1926 the Century Furniture Company of Grand Rapids, Michigan, published this basic treatise on period furniture. The company, with a team of premier craftsmen working with wood from all over the world, advertised that they could reproduce most any piece of furniture featured in this book.

Beginning with the Egyptian and Greek Age and running through the Early American era, 25 different periods are explored. Five hundred years of distinctively different styles, shapes, lines, decorations, legs, and finials make this quick reference an added tool for beginners as well as those considered experts in the field of period furniture.

The chronology of furniture styles on pages 150 through 152 is an education within itself and takes the guesswork out of dating period furniture. The glossary on pages 153 – 158 featuring 120 terms relative to furniture will broaden your knowledge on the subject.

With over 150 actual photographs of furniture and nearly 100 line drawings of shapes, finials, legs, and decorations, this book further adds to your education pertaining to antique furniture.

Keep in mind that this book was first printed in 1926 by a company that reproduced antique furniture in every detail. So, let the buyer beware.

FOREWORD

An acquaintance with the romance, the culture and the contemporaneous events which caused the birth and the development of period styles in furniture cannot but lead to a better appreciation of modern furnishings — the furniture of one's home, and the homes of one's friends. In covering briefly the more prominent furniture eras in history, it is our hope that this book will enable the reader to find in his own surroundings a wealth of heretofore hidden beauty at once interesting and stimulating.

PREFACE

G ENERALLY speaking, the American people as a whole are acquiring a better appreciation of the beauty and refining influences of good furniture.

This rather broad statement is accurate in that it reflects the cultural growth of our nation. Modern taste in furniture, as in music and in literature, is founded upon a fairly wide-spread understanding of fundamentals.

Good furniture (not necessarily expensive furniture) is furniture designed along certain lines of harmony and symmetry which will be beautiful always. And furniture so designed is independent of transitory style preferences. It has a reason for living, even after a temporary popular demand may have ceased.

Today, the better pieces of furniture may be reproductions of the earlier masterpieces, or they may be intelligent modern adaptations of certain historic styles. It is this historic significance embodied in a piece of furniture that makes the study of furniture absorbing to the layman; and makes the ownership of good furniture gratifying to the home-builder.

It is of small significance whether the present popularity of "period" furniture grew out of a unanimous cultural revolt against the furnishings of the past century, or developed from small beginnings by a few of the better makers, aided and encouraged by the enlightened taste of the more sophisticated buyers.

But this is true: that "period" has become a name to conjure with in furniture circles. And since this book is devoted chiefly to a study of the various periods, the word deserves definition as applied to furniture.

Period furniture is nothing more or less than that furniture which was favored, or obtained popularity, during a certain historical era in a certain country.

In the beginning, furniture invariably was utilitarian in its purpose. Embellishments followed as a natural desire of human beings to make more attractive that with which they lived. The shifting tastes and vogues in furniture styles were occasioned by many influences.

The ascendency to the throne of a new monarch frequently marked the beginning of a new era in furniture and decorative styles, because the people were quick to accept any type that had received royal favor. In England during the 18th Century, however, several designers were so outstanding that their names, instead of the names of the reigning monarchs, now identify their productions.

Religion played a very important rôle in the changes in furniture styles. So did politics. Certain feminine influences at court were responsible for characteristic designs, patterns and color schemes. Frequently, travelers returning from foreign countries brought back new ideas of exotic art, which either received popular favor or were adopted and employed by the artists and the craftsmen of the day.

Always there was more or less blending of period styles. The designers of one country borrowed freely from the designers of another. Foreign ideas were adapted to native tastes; and as a result, the best thought of many countries frequently are combined. This in itself makes difficult the identification of certain very fine pieces of furniture; for indeed, one may find an Italian piece designed in the manner of the French, who in turn had been influenced largely by English or Spanish designers. Motifs were adopted and adapted, influenced always by the racial preferences and social life of the people.

Then, too, there was always an intermixture of styles during the transitional periods as tastes changed. An outstanding example of this is noticed in the transition from the sturdy William and Mary style to the lighter and more feminine Queen Anne, in which elements of both styles are gracefully incorporated.

Notwithstanding this commingling of artistic thought and its interpretation in various woods, furniture styles and periods are quite well defined and classified.

Modern furniture draws its inspiration liberally from the past and adds the ingenuity of modern craftsmanship and modern machinery, together with all that modern designing has learned from the Golden past.

To accomplish all this, however, requires intelligent study, innate ability, creative imagination, excellent craftsmanship and the will to do. Lumber and machinery cannot substitute for the human mind, even in a day of quantity production. And it is this human element that has made the inanimate products of the Century Furniture Company of Grand Rapids, Michigan, fit to live and to endure.

As a true exponent of high ideals and qualifications, more and more has the name *Century —Grand Rapids* become synonymous with all that is best in furniture throughout America. Authentic reproductions of the best designs the past can offer, intelligent application of the more pleasing motifs by which the furniture of various periods is identified, extremely discriminating and comprehensive selection of woods, finishes and upholstery, together with unsurpassed cabinetmaking and loving craftsmanship—these are the fundamentals upon which every *Century* piece is built.

Tables, chairs, stools, sofas, window-seats, cabinets, deep luxurious overstuffed pieces, together with living room, dining room and bedroom furniture, and library combinations are included in the products from Grand Rapids bearing the *Century* Shopmark.

GRAND RAPIDS
THE FURNITURE CAPITAL OF AMERICA

G RAND RAPIDS did not become the furniture capital of America by accident. The growth of Grand Rapids to a position of dominance in the furniture world, and in the minds of intelligent persons throughout the world, is the result of high ideals combined with superior workmanship in its productions.

Yesterday, Grand Rapids was a small woodworking center because the supply of raw materials was close at hand. Today, Grand Rapids' position in the furniture world is synonymous with that of Paris as the arbiter of fashions in women's dress, the supremacy of Sheffield in steel, Limoges in china, Belfast in linens, Nuremberg in toys, Amsterdam in diamonds. And today the furniture made and sold in Grand Rapids is constructed of woods that are cut from the forests of the entire world.

But Grand Rapids' furniture is made of more than wood. It is more than expert cabinet making. It is even more than artistic lines and expert designing. Grand Rapids has gained and retained its supremacy because its pioneer manufacturers set their standards high; because succeeding generations of furniture manufacturers have maintained an ideal; because *quality* and quality plus production, has been the distinguishing characteristic of Grand Rapids' contribution to the betterment of furniture, and the homes for which it is designed.

PERIODS AND STYLES

HUNDREDS of volumes have been published on furniture and furniture styles. They have been written by archaeologists, furniture lovers, collectors and historians; and the subject has been covered from practically all angles, and at great length.

But in offering this treatise, it is hoped that the various styles and periods may be briefly summarized and classified, so that the reader may easily acquaint himself with the dominating motifs found in modern furniture, and may be able to find in present-day pieces a background for their existence.

Although furniture is essentially utilitarian in its purpose, every age since the dawn of civilization has sought to make chairs more than things to sit upon; to make tables more than boards to hold food; to make beds and chests more beautiful than necessary for the sole purposes of sleeping and the storing of clothing or household articles. Every age has ornamented and embellished its furniture in proportion to its own cultural limitations, its social, religious or political restrictions.

A period is an era of time in which there is a dominating influence. History reveals the fact that this influence invariably affects the style of architecture, decoration, textiles, pottery and other articles. And always has furniture reflected the modes and manners of the times, the tastes of the people, the conditions under which they were living, the influences which were paramount at the time.

The influences responsible for a period, so called, may fall under three headings: Classic, Oriental, and Gothic or Christian. Classic means restraint. Oriental means sensuousness, material expression, full license, much color and warmth. Gothic or Christian means symbolism, imagination.

Religion, politics, social conditions: these determining factors may be recognized by their influence on each period. And period art becomes crystallized when the art of a people is dominated by the same set of influences. Radical changes in conditions — changes that affect a people — create a new period.

A resumé of furniture styles would begin somewhere around the 16th Century. There is little of interest to the student of furniture prior to this time, insofar as furniture itself is concerned. But there is interest in these earlier days because of the wealth of inspiration they provided for succeeding ages. Egyptian art, the flourishing eras of Greek and Roman art, the Byzantine, Moorish and Saracenic styles of decoration all contributed their share. And yet the motifs borrowed from these countries at different times usually were not decorations of furniture, but were found in architecture, rugs, jewelry, etc.

EGYPTIAN

The Egyptian Period from 5,000 B.C. to 500 A.D. concerns a people who possessed a dominant idea. Every Egyptian believed his soul was an atom of the king. Thus did Egyptians build tombs, and turn all their science and art to the preservation of soul and body. The supposed decorative effects of the Egyptians are not decorations in the true sense. They are the hieroglyphic lives of their builders, and so colorful and effective that they become decorative. The distinctive art of this nation has not been lost to succeeding ages in furniture, as many interesting examples prove.

GREEK

Evolute

Greek life, history and mythology are generally known. Greek art was a development of the pure classic. The perfection of the body was an ideal. Out of Greek art has grown Greek proportion. All Greek ornament is aesthetic in principle, and carries the perfection of pure form to a point that has never been equalled. The naturalistic was disregarded for the development of a correct proportion of abstract shapes, forms, etc. Greek art represents restraint. Ornamentation becomes decorative because it is used to emphasize structure. The Greeks chose decorative material in harmony with the object they were to decorate. They embodied the spirit first. Needless to say, the influence of Greek art upon the Renaissance was all powerful; and its influence will be everlasting.

Greek Key

Ancient Roman Bronze and Marble Table, now in the Metropolitan Museum of Art.

Photograph of the oldest wooden chair in America, made in Egypt more than 3,500 years ago. The white spots on the back are inlays of bone and ivory.

Pompeian Arm Chair, made of maple, painted black, with black patent leather seat. The top rail is painted in old red with typical decorations in color. (A Century adaptation.)

Greek Table made of bronze. The table edge shows a band of lions pursuing stags. (Photograph of the original in the Metropolitan Museum of Art.)

A carved oak credence with panels in old reds, blues, and whites. The hinges, lock-plate and handles are of wrought iron.

Fifteenth century Seigneurial chair in carved oak. Note the linen fold motif on the apron and back.

A Gothic chest of splendid, architectural lines. It belongs to the Fifteenth Century and is in carved oak with wrought iron hinges, rings and corner plates.

ROMAN

As from Greek art, furniture also has drawn motifs and ideals from Roman art as expressed in architecture. Contrary to the Greek aesthetic idea, Roman development centered about an appeal to the senses; a gratification of self, a desire to spend. Ornamentation was naturalistic and prodigal. Roman designers adopted the Doric, Ionic and Corinthian of the Greek orders and added one of their own. Roman art was original only in its development of the Greek. Romans fitted it to their time, added to it, and in many cases overdid it. The "egg-and-dart" motif, the acanthus leaf, and the anthemion, or Greek honeysuckle, have been favorite ornaments for all furniture designers who reproduce the Classic.

Patera

GOTHIC

Egg and Dart

Following the fall of Rome, when all of Europe was torn by invasion and conflict, there ensued that stagnant period known as the Dark Ages. During this time no art was developed in architecture or anything else. The individual was subordinate to the church and life on earth was but a preparation for life hereafter. Christianity—although misinterpreted—had claimed the entire thought of man. The Crusades began. The idea of a Heaven and Hell, with a world between, was new. Religion was the dominating note of life. Individual initiative was submerged, and thinking suppressed.

In this atmosphere of religious fervor, when the Crusaders were returning from foreign lands with fresh ideas, the period known as "Gothic" developed. It lasted from 1100 to 1500—400 years. Where the Greeks had sought bodily perfection, and the Romans sensual pleasure, the Gothic period was marked by the demotion of the body for the advancement of the soul. Paganism was denied; the art that developed was deeply spiritual, impressively symbolical. And the church remained all powerful.

Quatrefoil

One sees, in the pointed arches and steepled towers, a reaching upward to Heaven. The flying-buttress of architecture, adopted later in furniture, signified man's leaning on God. The familiar Gothic circle interprets the eternal love of God; the trefoil stood for the Trinity; the quatrefoil for the four Apostles; the cinquefoil for the five Epistles; the ivy leaf for man's frailty and clinging to God; the oak leaf for the strength of God; the dove for peace, heart atonement and the Cross triumphant; and the familiar linen-fold represented the cloth used to cover the Host. The style originated in France, but was soon seized upon by other countries in Europe.

Art and decoration reflect a people, and thus did the art and decoration of the Gothic period but reflect the thoughts, the manners, and the modes of these people. "As a man thinks," one might say, will apply to furniture of the ages.

Linen Fold

Furniture of the time naturally took its keynote from the churches, for it was here that thought centered. Thus on Gothic furniture, so called, is found carving and ornamentation peculiarly ecclesiastical.

The style was essentially perpendicular. straight-line, and the architectural proportions were splendidly impressive with high, awe-inspiring, soaring lines. Oak was a favorite wood in interior construction and furnishing.

Generally speaking, modern homes cannot accommodate Gothic furniture. Church pulpits, pews and stalls retain the motifs, the severity of outline, and massiveness of contour. Here is found their greatest adaptability. The period is important, because the Renaissance which followed indicated a swing of the pendulum in a direction exactly opposite to ecclesiastical influence and religious submersion of the people.

Gothic Tracery

ITALIAN RENAISSANCE
1443 - 1564

UNLESS one has some familiarity with the political and social conditions of Europe prior to the 15th Century, the Renaissance has little significance. But when one appreciates the conditions under which the people of the Middle Ages had been living, it is readily understood why public sentiment was bound to swing away from the ascetic era of religious restriction and dominance by the church, to one less severe.

Acanthus Leaf

The term Renaissance means re-birth. It marked the real awakening of art, literature and life to more human ideals. As early as 1300, people began to rebel against fasting, prayer and penance.

In the years that followed they reverted to the arts of Greece and Rome; they read Roman plays that had been dead for a thousand years— in fact they dared do things which for many years previously had been punishable almost by death. Thus, Greek and Roman ideals and ideas were born again—but to a different people.

The Renaissance began and developed in Italy. It spread throughout Europe. Italian artists were imported to English shores. As the Crusaders were conquered by Byzantine arts, so was Charles VIII of France conquered by the wonders of the Renaissance craftsmen when he

Italian Buffet, Sixteenth Century, Florence—A reproduction of an antique in the Metropolitan Museum of Art in New York City. The rich carving is a Renaissance type of decoration, and is pleasingly balanced.

A dignified, richly carved Italian 17th Century Chair—This type originated in the state of Lombardy.

Venetian Chair in old green crackle lacquer and gold.

Fifteenth Century Book Shelves of carved and inlaid walnut. The cupboard door has an antique painted iron grille over damask.

Note the square effect of this 15th Century Italian Straight Chair. The uprights always extended above the back and terminated in carved finials. Square high seats had fringed seat rails.

Florentine Coffee Stand of walnut with marble top.

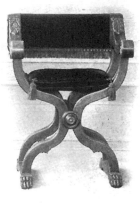

Reproduction of an Italian Chest of Drawers.

Reproduction of an Italian Folding Chair of old walnut covered in velvet.

Italian Renaissance Table, displaying the wealth of naturalistic motifs and marvelous carving that marked the revival.

A highly decorative Venetian mirror with frame of carved and gilded wood.

Venetian. A console table in carved wood, painted old biscuit with floral decorations. The carved ornaments are finished in burnished gold.

invaded Italy. To Paris he, also, brought Italian artists. Louis XII brought them to Touraine, and Francis I to Fontainebleau. The Renaissance spread across the Pyrenees into Spain, as it crossed the Alps into Germany, Flanders and the Netherlands.

The Renaissance is divided into three stages: First: the Early Renaissance between 1350 and 1400. Second: the High Renaissance from 1400 to 1500; and Third: the Decadent Period between 1500 and 1600. The main sources of this new movement in Italy were in Florence, Rome, Venice, Milan and Lombardy, and the styles of furniture emanating from these various centers show the marks of colloquial interpretation.

Guilloche

Naturally, the Renaissance ideals rejected the pointed arch, the long vertical lines and other distinctly characteristic details of former Gothic structures. They rejected Gothic symbolism. The Classic ornamentation of Greece and Rome was revived. Thus came into life again the honeysuckle, lotus, egg-and-dart, acanthus, bead-moldings, the Greek-fret, rosettes, medallions, cupids, griffins, etc. Long horizontal lines, with plain exteriors, unbroken and massive, palatial in size and in effect, substantially solid, with beautiful proportions and artistically restrained, were outstanding characteristics.

Spool Bead

The principal wood was walnut, while the upholstery was largely of crimson velvet with gold fringe, tassels and nails; although leather also was used extensively.

Wood carving was one of the great glories of the early centuries. Italy not only left a wealth of wonderfully carved furniture to posterity, but added to it the warm colorings of a distinctive native taste.

Finial

Colors are an integral part of Italian art; and the clever craftsmen of the time, when they could not get woods of fine quality, used paint and gold to overcome the deficiencies. The style therefore quickly became florid. Skilled carvers being too few to meet the demand for carved motifs, plastic ornament was resorted to and was produced from various molds. Gesso, a plastic ornament, was developed, and later Gesso Duro, a hard plastic substitute for carving, also was employed.

From Rome, the cradle of the baroque, from Milan, Genoa, Naples, Venice, Tuscany, Lombardy, Bologna, Verona, and various villas came furniture for more than 500 years—all Italian, but ever influenced by local and foreign manners, customs and conditions; religious, social and political affairs. Venice, city of gaiety and fashion, reflected in her furniture styles, the frivolous, flirtatious and voluptuous life of the upper classes during the eighteenth century. Bright, feminine colors, rococo scrolls and graceful painted decorations were favored. Indeed the age was comparable with the contemporary conditions in France under Louis XV. Brescia, like many Italian villas, distinguished by simplicity of form, its lack of ornament in relief—color decorations that fully compensated for the absence of finer materials.

Louis XIII Bench

*French Renaissance Hearth Seat—The elaborate carvings
of the period are suggested.*

*French Renaissance Table of old mahogany and gold
with amaranth wood top.*

Louis (XIII) Treize—Middle of the Seventeenth Century.

FRENCH RENAISSANCE
1515 - 1643

FRANCE, like Italy and other countries in Western Europe, soon began to feel the effects of the Renaissance. In spite of the fact that the Gothic styles were of French origin, its native art, tradition and restraint were left behind in the re-birth of the classic. In fact, the Renaissance influenced France to a marvelous extent. Wars which resulted in expeditions to Italy brought France in touch with the styles to be found there; and in this way the new taste was brought back to France. Designers also were imported from Italy.

Caryatid

France was a united country under Francis I. The style in furniture and in decoration was set by the court and completely dominated the country. The situation was different in Italy. Different parts of the latter country were controlled by independent dukes and princes, and this resulted in varying interpretations.

The style of furniture in France, however, was quite similar to the Italian Renaissance, although it was far more elaborately carved. It is quite evident that much Gothic feeling remained, manifested in the characteristic structural proportions. Lines were straight and rectangular, but softened by the very rich decoration. All this imparted a feeling of architectural solidity. The general effect was one of weight and richness.

Carving was the prominent element of ornamentation. It was of the finest and most elaborate nature, much of it being almost sculptured. The motifs, though classic, were much freer and more natural than those employed by the Italians. The acanthus leaf was used liberally; also the French royal insignia, such as the fleur-de-lis and the porcupine. Other motifs were fluted columns, sphinxes, lion heads, human heads and figures, or caryatides. Small insets of black marble were typical of the style.

Bun Foot

One of the distinguishing marks between the Italian and the French Renaissance styles was the pendant ornament used in the French pieces, a survival of the Gothic feeling. The arms and backs of chairs, usually straight, rectangular and uncomfortable in appearance, were quite Gothic in effect except for the Renaissance carving, while the feet were block, bun or pear-shaped.

Walnut was used extensively by the French at this time. It was ideally adapted to the fine carved styles.

Typical French Renaissance furniture is too massive and too ornate for many modern homes, but the style lends itself to other modern requirements, and is responsible for many beautiful reproductions.

SPANISH RENAISSANCE
1500 - 1650

THE revival of learning in Spain was influenced to a great extent by Moorish art,
and many Spanish pieces of even a later period
betray this feeling. Spain, in the early part of
the 16th Century, was attaining the height of
its glory. Charles V, King of Spain, was also
Emperor of the Netherlands, Austria, Germany
and Italy, and a powerful monarch was he.
America had been discovered by Columbus.
The Renaissance was general.

For several centuries prior to the Renaissance,
however, a large part of Spain had been occupied
by the Mohammedan Moors from Northern
Africa. Already had they been overcome and
expelled; but the influence of their art remained
stamped indelibly upon the country. Combined
with this Moorish influence were the Gothic and
the styles of other countries. Italy's influence
was marked. This intermixture of artistic conception resulted in furniture that possessed a
character distinctly different from any other
style in Europe.

Dignity and richness; restrained, yet vigorous
decorations were outstanding characteristics.
Spanish furniture was of splendid and honest
character. It possessed great individuality, bal-

Shell

Spanish Turning

ance of porportion and refinement, together with wealth and brilliance of color in relief against severe backgrounds.

Intricate scrolls and arcades, as well as the twisted iron braces on tables, were distinctly Spanish; but much of the beautiful leather and iron work, so identified with Spanish furniture, shows the Moorish taste. The typical "Spanish Scroll" foot, however, was taken from the Netherlands during the Spanish occupation. It later spread to England, and the same idea was carried out on the furniture of Colonial America. The claw-foot, frequently found in Spanish furniture, as well as the hoof-foot, shows a general Renaissance influence. Other feet found during this period were the bun-shaped, the pear-shaped, the straight and rectangular.

All Spanish ornament was rich and profuse. The carving was fine, and the curves subtle. Elaborate metal motifs used in decoration, and the intricate open-work designs, frequently under-laid with red velvet, were essentially Spanish. The use of gilt nails was quite characteristic, and frequently a design was formed by these nail-heads. Inlaying was a distinctive style. Bone, brass, silver and tortoise-shell were used. A Spanish style was the use of leather over wood; and this leather was stamped, colored and highlighted in various intricate designs. Arcades of spindles also were prominent, this motif having been borrowed from Spanish architecture.

The shell ornament, which later was employed most generously in many countries, was used in

Spanish Desk of the 17th Century—Made of walnut, but the top is of antique leather, and the edge studded with brass nails. The carvings are in antique gold, and the wrought iron stretcher is painted red.

Spanish Desk Chair of walnut with ebonized spindles, antique leather seat and back top. The wrought iron stretcher is painted red.

Spanish Arm Chair of carved and painted walnut. It is finished in patine, to impart an antique effect.

Spanish Buffet of the 17th Century. Note the typical carving in walnut.

Spanish Cabinet of old red lacquer with partly raised decorations on a carved and gilded walnut base. Note the wrought metal decoration and the prominent shell motif.

Spanish Love Seat—Made of carved walnut and gilded. The stretcher is painted wrought iron.

Spanish Chairs. The shell motifs, the Spanish scroll foot, decorative brass nail heads and other typically Castilian details are apparent.

Spain at this time due to the fact that the shell was a symbol of St. James, the Patron Saint of the country. Decorating surfaces by means of applied moldings originated in this Spanish era. This style also migrated to the Netherlands and then to England, where it became a distinctive mark of the late Jacobean Period during the reign of Charles II, more than a century later.

Fret

In spite of the fact that the Moors were people who used little furniture, whose idea of decoration was principally by means of elaborate hangings and architectural ornament, many Moresque and Spanish pieces were the ancestors of furniture that became popular in other countries.

Spanish pieces were not plentiful, and the variety was comparatively small. A characteristic of the tables was the trestle-like appearance of the legs. They usually splayed outward and were connected by a wrought-metal brace of graceful design. Chairs, upholstered benches, beds, tables and unique types of writing desks, together with certain chests and screens, comprised the greater part of the early Spanish furnishings.

Spanish Foot

Recently, there has been a revival of interest in Spanish furniture for modern homes. While the typical Spanish room is rather dignified and austere, the virile designs and warmth of colors make this style admirably adapted to some of the more pretentious modern homes; and, with proper restraint, this old world atmosphere may be imparted even to the smaller dwelling.

DUTCH AND FLEMISH RENAISSANCE
16TH AND 17TH CENTURIES

THE influence of the Italian Renaissance reached the Netherlands and resulted in an architecture and an art known as Flemish Renaissance. To understand the Dutch and Flemish styles, however, one must take into consideration the history of the times.

Spiral Twist

Holland and Flanders were not separate countries until the middle of the 17th Century. Up to that time the general character of their furniture was similar. For years, however, Holland had been ruled by Spain, and had been for centuries involved in wars against foreign oppression. In 1581 Holland declared herself a Republic and became separate from Flanders, which still remained under Spanish rule. Styles in furniture and architecture then changed. Holland developed a style of her own; and Flanders followed French fashions.

Holland was a great seafaring nation at this time. Her travelers brought back new materials and new ideas from Japan, the East Indies and various other countries. It is easy to realize, therefore, how the influences of Spain, Italy, France, Germany and the Orient were intermingled in the development of the Dutch style.

Flemish Chair of carved and polychromed walnut. Spanish influence is here noted in the arcades of spindles. The side posts of the back show both Spanish and Italian influence.

Flemish Cabinet illustrating the elaborate, fine carving of the Flemish craftsmen. The ornaments are classic, while the carved acanthus leaves and lions' heads are Renaissance motifs.

Early Eighteenth Century Dutch Chairs in highly polished green lacquer, decorated with typical flowers and figures in color.

Late Seventeenth Century Sideboard in walnut with elaborately decorated front of flowers, foliage and figures in colored marquetry. The top is inlaid with bands of oyster shell veneer. The conspicuous cabriole legs are a mark of the style.

In turn, all these influences affected English furniture: directly, because England shared Holland's passion for exploration; but more particularly as a result of the exile of Charles II in the Netherlands, and the rise of William of Orange to the English throne. From these sources developed what is known as the Late Jacobean (including the Carolean) and William and Mary periods.

The Flemish craftsmen employed oak as the material for their furniture. The distinguishing feature was a profusion of elaborate carvings, and, because the Dutch were very fond of flowers, floral designs of exceeding beauty were found in many elaborate inlays.

Holland and Flanders were home-loving countries. Their furniture reflected a solid domesticity, often heavy and bulky and frequently more clumsy than graceful. Although it may be considered inferior to the Renaissance styles of other countries, its proportions were good, and no doubt in close harmony with the architectural character of the homes and interiors in which it was placed.

Flemish Scroll

ELIZABETHAN PERIOD
1558 - 1603

Rosette

THE Elizabethan Period was, actually, the English Renaissance. Henry VIII, the preceding monarch, possessed a love for the beautiful. He invited artisans from all over Europe to visit and beautify the English Court. His invitation was readily accepted by artists and craftsmen from Spain and the Netherlands, who were glad to find a haven in England from the wars of their respective lands.

During the succeeding reign of Elizabeth art, as well as styles in architecture and furniture, flourished. English navigators embarked on many voyages of discovery and conquest. This was the age of Shakespeare. It was, in every sense of the word, a real revival of learning, a great and glorious period.

Channelling

In the styles which predominated was an intermixture of French, Italian and Flemish influences, spread over a background of Tudor tastes and the lingering characteristics of the Gothic.

Inasmuch as the English Renaissance followed the English Gothic, one finds the furniture of the period massive, straight in line, elaborately carved and largely copied from the Italian Renaissance. The furniture was made of oak,

An Elizabethan cabinet in oak. The interior is fitted with shelves and a desk, the sliding writing bed of which is inlaid with leather. The doors are decorated with inlaid panels.

An Elizabethan table with top panelled in Pollard oak. The inlaid work of yellow, black and green woods on the rails and apron is characteristic of the period.

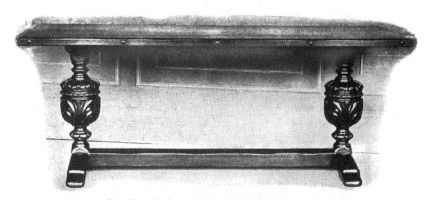

*Late Sixteenth Century Elizabethan Tables of Walnut—
The table above is octagonal with a panelled top of Pollard
oak, while the refectory table below is panelled with English
oak. The bulbous ornaments are typically Elizabethan. The
low, heavy stretchers are characteristic. Note how the
stretcher has been made to present a worn appearance.*

and the richly carved ornament covered rather elaborately the sturdy English structure, comprising what might be considered the most dignified and impressive of all English styles.

There is an excuse for the heaviness and clumsiness of Tudor furniture. One must consider the type of houses in which this furniture was placed, and the habits and the manners of the men and women who lived therein. At the time of Henry VIII, for instance, a man dressed in full armour required a chair or bench that was sturdy almost to the point of massiveness. Then, too, the Great Hall of medieval Europe was so huge that even the largest furniture seemed small in comparison.

Melon Bulb

During the reign of Elizabeth, a tendency toward the lightening of furniture became apparent. The long rectangular dining table, which existed from medieval days through the Elizabethan Period, filled a purpose. The host and guest sat on one side of the table only, while the serving was done from the other. In this martial age, such an arrangement enabled the master to sit at a point of vantage, in case of sudden attack.

The more outstanding motifs of the Elizabethan Period were the carved acanthus leaves of the Italian Renaissance, the Tudor arch and the Tudor rose—a symbol from the War of the Roses—carved lozenges, the linen-fold panel of the Gothic, fruit and floral carvings, grotesque figures nude to the waist, animals, masques and heraldic devices. The ornamentation consisted chiefly of carvings, moldings and paneling, very rich in effect. Pierced carving is not observed. Bulbous ornaments on legs and balusters were often used, and carving was spread well over the surfaces.

Among the characteristic pieces of furniture of the time were the huge four-poster beds. (Shakespeare's reference to the "Great Bed of Ware" concerned an Elizabethan style.) Wainscot chairs, long rectangular tables, cupboards, chests, stools, benches and court-cupboards were in vogue. The last mentioned does not mean a cupboard used by royalty, but is derived from the French word "court" meaning short.

Pure Elizabethan furniture is almost too medieval in effect and too strictly architectural for modern homes; yet an intelligent employment of modified Elizabethan motifs is still used very successfully to some extent.

Pilaster

JACOBEAN PERIOD
1603 - 1688

THE term, "Jacobean," actually includes three or more periods. It is derived from King James I, the Latin for which is Jacobus. The First or Early Jacobean Period, from 1603 to 1649, includes the reigns of James I and Charles I. The Second Period, known as Cromwellian or Commonwealth, lasted from 1649 to 1660, the time during which Oliver Cromwell was Lord Protector of England. The Late Jacobean, or the Third Period of the Jacobean era, comprised the reigns of Charles II and James II. That of Charles II also is called the Late Stuart, the Restoration or the Carolean Period, and there was considerable variation of the general style during the time these monarchs ruled.

Lunette

Each of the three periods should be considered in turn, with ample time given to the varying influences that were manifested during the latter part of this century. The Early Jacobean and the Late Jacobean are very different in every way, and it is quite necessary to understand these distinctions. The furniture of this time is probably the most difficult to classify because of the influence of the many conflicting political and social events of the time.

The Early Jacobean Period was developed from the Elizabethan. It was similar to it in its general styles and proportions, but was much more subdued. The ornament was less pronounced, particularly in the curves and curved flourishes which had been the glory of the Elizabethan Period. The style was straighter; it was much more practical, more simple, and tended to grace rather than to strength.

Bannister Back

The proportions of the Early Stuart, or Jacobean, were rectangular and low. This lowness was accounted for by the low ceilings of the time. Legs were straight, and turned in various designs, but the "melon-bulb" was smaller, if used at all. The underbracing of chairs and tables always tied the legs together; and, as in the Elizabethan Period, served definitely as foot rests, although quite close to the floor. Ornaments were heavy and consisted mostly of carvings. The effect imparted to the flat surfaces was more monotonous than the Elizabethan. And as in the preceding period, there was an intermixture of Renaissance with Gothic art.

Some Early Jacobean chairs find favor in modern homes, and certain tables carry a historic charm; but generally speaking it is the Later Jacobean style which finds favor today.

Scrolled Arm

It must be understood that these styles in furniture, and interior furnishings did not and could not change with such rapidity as, for instance, the changes in modern dress. They were more or less the result of a sentiment that manifested itself over a long period of years. Thus, styles of the Elizabethan Period, or the

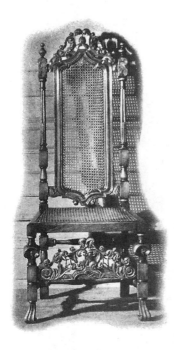

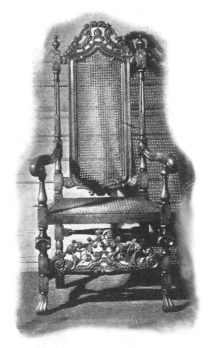

Late Jacobean Chairs, typical of the period. Caning became popular at this time. A Flemish and Dutch influence is betrayed in this style.

Wainscot Chair of carved oak (antiqued). The back panels are inlaid with flower forms of black and yellow in a conventionalized design.

Welsh Dresser—Came into use during the Commonwealth days of England. The lower part was a cupboard or drawers, while the open shelves above were used for the display of utensils.

Jacobean Arm Chair—Dip seat caned.

Upholstered Jacobean Arm Chair (late).

A Jacobean chest of carved oak with wrought iron hinges and a panelled top. A wealth of decorative motifs are apparent here.

Jacobean Escritoire with secret compartments, which served as a repository for valuables.

An English arm chair in oak typical of the Seventeenth Century.

Jacobean Carved Oak Desk.

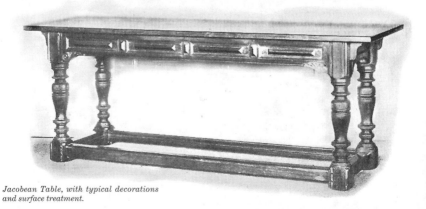

Jacobean Table, with typical decorations and surface treatment.

English Renaissance, really began to be felt in England during the reign of James I. But gradually this style was modified as has been pointed out.

James I died and Charles I was executed.

Then came Cromwell, a hater of Aristocracy, and puritanically religious. A new style resulted. Obviously, the spirit of the times tended toward Democracy, and furniture displayed an austere and simple severity. The people, in their mode of living, banished luxury and frivolity; and the furniture, as is always the case, reflected this trend.

The lines of all pieces were straight. The general effect was plain. Proportions were square and rectangular. The bulbous legs, so characteristic of Elizabethan and Early Jacobean styles, were out of fashion. Bun or ball feet remained in style, however, due to the Dutch influence of the time. Underbracing was generally used, and was stout in effect; but turned underbracing began to come into use.

Oak still was the favored wood, but the extravagant decoration of the preceding period was frowned upon and only simple turnings and moldings were to be found. It was at this time that upholstery began to find a more general use. Chairs frequently had padded backs, as well as padded seats. Somber-colored materials and leather were selected for this purpose.

S–Scroll

The gateleg table is not strictly Cromwellian, but it originated in England at that time and has been a popular piece of furniture ever since. It is typically English. Other furniture of the Commonwealth Period that has been retained for its picturesqueness is the Welsh Dresser and the typical Cromwellian chair.

In spite of the fact that England was quite glad to be rid of Charles I, the English felt a desire for the pomp of royalty. They were rather tired of the dull, heavy life imposed upon them. With the return of Charles II and the restoration of the Stuart line, there occurred a strong reaction in the manners and modes of the English people. Charles II had been an exile in Flanders during Cromwell's incumbency. He had formed certain artistic tastes during his wanderings in foreign lands, and he brought back with him many new thoughts when he ascended the throne.

"C" Scrolls

The stern frugality of the Cromwellian times gave way to a gayety and luxury that betrayed, particularly in its furniture, many foreign influences, to-wit: French, Dutch, Flemish, Spanish, Portuguese and Italian. The principal ornamental motifs of the Carolean Period were the "S" and "C" scrolls, which were repeated and reiterated, joined and rejoined, until they finally completed a panel. The style is recognized by its ornamentation, by its spiral turned legs, and its geometrical moldings.

And, though handicapped for want of the turning lathe which had enabled the Dutch woodworkers to bring the spiral to such a high degree of perfection, the English cabinetmakers soon acquired great skill. Into prominence, at

Late Jacobean Bench of walnut with carvings in antique gold.

English Seventeenth Century—High upholstered backs were first used at this time. They were slanted backwards more than in previous styles. The arms and legs show the Flemish scrolls. The carved and scrolled front stretcher is a mark of the style.

Typical of the high padded back chairs of the time of Charles II. Foreign influences are apparent in this design.

Charles II settee with shaped and divided backs and carved walnut under framing. These were known as "courting" chairs.

this time, came the marvelous wood carver, Grinling Gibbons, who has ever been the glory and the despair of all wood carvers.

Motifs often used by the wood carvers of the day were roses, graceful acanthus leaves, scrolls and carved crowns; this last symbolizing the restoration of the monarchy. The square leather-covered chair-backs, which came into popularity, were copied from the Portuguese and introduced in compliment to the queen, Catherine of Braganza, a daughter of the royal house of Portugal.

It takes but little effort on the part of the investigator to trace the various national influences brought to bear on this period; but England absorbed them all, and wedded them to a national taste. Chairs and settees became gorgeously upholstered in fine needlepoint, velvet, or brocade. Daybeds, which had been banished by Cromwell, returned. High, upholstered chair-backs were used for the first time. There was a general desire for comfort and pleasure.

Grinling Gibbons Carving

Gambling with cards became the vogue; and this, coupled with the fact that tea, coffee and cocoa had been added to the beverages of England, led to a demand for smaller and lighter tables than had been the fashion. So great was this national desire for games, and so earnestly did the people seek merry companionship, that by the end of the 18th Century the importance of the card-table cannot be over-estimated. In fact, all the later-day designers left marvelous examples of exquisitely designed game-tables, which obviously were more of a luxury than a necessity.

It is impossible to over-estimate the growing influence of the magnificent French Court upon English life and manners of the day. Charles II was upon the closest terms of intimacy with Louis XIV, receiving a handsome pension from that monarch. English art was constantly being enriched by the genius of great French designers and craftsmen who journeyed freely from one court to the other.

Pendant

The Jacobean style and its various branches is popular today. The earlier designs have their uses principally as ornamental units, while the later Jacobean pieces find wide acceptance.

Charles II was succeeded by the second James, who was very unpopular. Conditions caused him to flee from the country, at which time his daughter Mary, who had married William of Holland, was invited to the throne.

WILLIAM AND MARY PERIOD
1688 - 1702 ENGLAND

THE style of William and Mary furniture always has been, and is today, one of the most popular in the modern home. Owing to its attractiveness and simple elegance, its appeal has been wide and it has proved highly desirable for modern environments.

Shaped Skirt

It has been mentioned previously how Mary, the daughter of James II who married William of Orange, was invited with her husband to return to England after the king had fled to France. These new rulers brought with them strong Dutch preferences, which were reflected in furniture. With them, of course, came large numbers of courtiers and workmen, who brought the styles of their own land.

England may have resented this invasion of Dutch taste; but the people were ready for a change. They were becoming tired of the Jacobean, so the more graceful Dutch styles appealed to them.

Carved Underbracing with Finial

Another important influence brought to bear on England at this time was the invasion of Huguenot craftsmen, who had been driven from France because of the revocation of the Edict of Nantes. This royal act deprived them of religious tolerance and subjected them to persecution. They were skilled textile workers and cabinetmakers and they did much to make the new styles an improvement over the old.

Mary was interested in house furnishings. She possessed good taste and was truly domestic. Her influence on styles and manners of the time was great. The interest then manifested for needlepoint work and embroideries of all kinds was due to her love of this art.

Octagonal Leg

For the first time, England was to know the beauty and comfort of a light and slender type of furniture. The William and Mary style was a complete revolution. It was subtle and graceful, a harmonious combination of straight and curved lines. The cabinet work was rectangular and arched; and double-arched backs on cabinets, as well as on the backs of settees and chairs, became a distinguishing feature. Individual pieces were made taller to harmonize with the increasing height of the ceilings.

The general effect of the furniture was very liveable, and the style is easily recognized. One may identify William and Mary furniture by the turned legs, with inverted cups; by the serpentine-shaped stretchers, usually crossed, and frequently with a finial at the intersection.

Inverted Cup

The backs of chairs were high and rounded at the top. Some of them were carved and caned or upholstered, and sometimes there was a combination of these methods. Backs were slanted somewhat and seats were square. The legs, which go so far toward identifying William

William and Mary Chair—Great attention was paid to upholstery and needlework at this time. A faithful adaptation in construction and contour.

William and Mary motifs are prominent on this cabinet—a lacquer box on a walnut stand. The hinges and lock plate are of antique etched brass.

Typical William and Mary Table of walnut. Inverted cup legs, carved bun feet, serpentine stretchers, and pendant pulls are of the period. The open carving was inspired by the Chinese ivories popular in England of that time.

*A beautifully gilded William and Mary box
with decorations in color, on a carved walnut
and cherry burl stand. The interior of the box
is silver lustre lacquer with decorations on the
doors.*

*William and Mary chair in carved wal-
nut. The seat rail is overlaid with cherry
burl.*

*William and Mary commode of carved walnut with
marquetry of cherry burl and various colored woods.
The top is Jaspe Oriental marble.*

and Mary pieces, were turned, octagonal, or square. The spiral-turned leg was a survival of the late Jacobean. Later in the period, the Dutch cabriole leg came into use. Feet were consistently the Dutch bun, the Dutch ball-and-claw, and the Spanish scroll, which was introduced to England through Holland, and not from Spain direct. Block-feet were found on low chests of drawers. Arms usually flared outward and were made of wood, or were upholstered and rolled over.

The Dutch cockle-shell motif was much favored. This was carried into the Queen Anne period later, and became an outstanding characteristic of that style. Another characteristic was the apron-shaped ornamentation with pendants. Marquetry was exceedingly popular, and veneering first began to be used largely.

The Dutch had brought a knowledge of lacquer from the Orient, and in England it became very much "the rage." Painting and gilding on the legs and underbracing were used, and rich color effects were popular. In fact, colors were very well liked. They were strong and vigorous; reds, blues and greens contrasting with the gilding. The colors in the upholstery and the painted and lacquered woods added greatly to the general effect.

Cabriole Leg—Hoof Foot

Characteristic pieces of the time were chairs and upholstered stools. Beds were exceedingly tall, with slender posts and elaborate hangings. Some of these posts were twice as high as a tall man. Chests of drawers appeared and became known as highboys and lowboys. China cabinets came into fashion, owing to the vogue for collecting china and ceramics which had been started by Queen Mary. Tall clocks appeared, elaborately decorated with marquetry. The long refectory type of table had gone out of style.

Walnut was the principal wood used. Some carving was employed, with the shell and acanthus leaf the favorite motifs; but inlay and marquetry were more popular.

Pear-Shaped Bulb on Leg

Daniel Marot, one of the more prominent designers during the reign of William and Mary was born in Paris about 1660. He was among the Protestant refugees who fled to the Netherlands upon the revocation of the Edict of Nantes by Louis XIV. Marot's father was an architect and engraver, from whom he received a great amount of his early training. Later he designed much of the furniture that was decorated by Andre-Charles Boulle, master of marquetry.

Marot entered the service of William of Orange, and in this capacity designed interiors and exteriors of merit. His style showed a subtle blending of French fundamentals with Dutch forms, and later when he became active in England, an element of British proportion entered his designing. He adopted the title of "Architect to the King of Great Britain."

QUEEN ANNE PERIOD
1702 - 1714 ENGLAND

Shaped Apron

THE style known as Queen Anne has been more often employed by modern furniture manufacturers than any other style. This, probably, is because the cabriole leg is one of the distinguishing features of this style. Therefore, any piece of furniture, no matter how inconsequential it might be, has been dubbed Queen Anne if it possessed anything resembling a cabriole leg. There is, however, a great deal more to this style of furniture than the shape of the legs; and only the more reputable cabinet-makers have been conscientious enough to create or reproduce Queen Anne furniture with all of its delicacy and gracefulness of line and its more subtle motifs. It must be said that the style forms the period of change between the heavy underbraced furniture of the earlier English periods, and the delicate style of the late Georgian makers.

Queen Anne, the daughter of James II who was forced to flee from England, came to the English throne upon the death of her brother-in-law, William of Orange. She possessed little taste or originality herself; but William already had made possible the continued ascendancy of the British Parliament. This forever ended the absolutism of the English monarchs, making

Cabriole Leg
Pad Foot

it quite possible for a style to flourish without royal sanction.

The distinctive William and Mary furniture, although a pleasing and popular style, did not long survive the monarchs for whom it was named. This short vogue was due, in the first place to the fact that the style was not truly British; in the second place, to the new ideas constantly put forward by British designers.

The Queen Anne period actually closes with the early Georgian when the powerful influence of the designer Chippendale began to be felt. In spite of the political intrigue of the time, national progress was being made and, notwithstanding the ill-feeling between England and France, certain style-influences crept in from that country.

Club Foot

The furniture of Queen Anne's time shows a step forward in refinement, in grace and in comfort. Probably it merely followed the ideals which the William and Mary furniture would have attained had its era been extended. The English home was becoming more modernized, and greater comforts began to be apparent. A review of Queen Anne furniture betrays this tendency, showing replacement of the more upright and uncomfortable chairs of the earlier period by the upholstered, overstuffed wing-chairs of the later days. The Queen Anne period also can be noted as the beginning of the "easy chair." It was known as the age of walnut be-cause this was the principal wood used and because it was in high favor.

It has been pointed out how various conditions influenced furniture styles. In the Queen Anne

*Queen Anne Wing Chair—The.
legs are of walnut.*

*Later Queen Anne Arm Chair.
The Dutch cabriole legs are not
connected by stretchers.*

A Queen Anne Love Seat.

*Reproduction of Queen Anne
mahogany arm chair.*

*Queen Anne upholstered desk chair
of carved walnut.*

*Reproduction of Queen Anne commode, carved,
and partially gilded. It is made of walnut.*

period, for instance, wide flaring chair seats came into style; principally because of the huge skirts women then wore. This accounts also for the fact that many types of chairs lacked arms. The desire for comfort is found in the backs of chairs, which were "spooned" to fit the body.

The cockle-shell carving was the most popular ornament. It is found on the knees of cabriole legs, on the cresting of chair backs, in the middle of drawers and aprons, and frequently formed the center motif of carved designs. This ornament and the cabriole leg are perhaps the most outstanding features of identification. The cabriole leg, however, is an adaptation of the "S" scroll or wave, or cymacurve; and the cyma curve is a definite characteristic of all Queen Anne furniture. It is to be found incorporated on the aprons, chair-backs, mirrors and even table tops.

Cyma Curves

The cabriole leg is an ancient type of support, and was brought to England from the Orient by Dutch designers. It will be seen how this type of leg was elaborately carved and used on Louis XV furniture, and how it also became a marked characteristic of the furniture of Chippendale. A variety of feet were used, the claw-and-ball, the paw, and the club leading in popularity.

The Queen Anne period was rather simple in ornamentation. Surfaces were kept plain, without paneling or molding. Veneering was much used and lacquer work was popular, whereas marquetry and inlay passed out of style. Upholstery was in high favor.

Double Hood Top

It will be remembered that the English home originally had been sparsely furnished. Never until this time did practically every type of furniture come into use. Small tables, which had become popular after the Cromwellian regime, were in extreme favor during Queen Anne's reign. Dining tables were of the drop-leaf variety; chests of drawers, highboys and lowboys, and beds with tall slender posts supporting testers, were very much the vogue. A characteristic feature of the chair was the solid fiddleback-shaped splat, with uprights in sweeping contours. These backs were generally narrow. Underbracing was not used.

Later designers used the Queen Anne construction and added much to it of their own conception. These later influences meet in what is known as the early Georgian period, a style similar to Queen Anne, showing the same Dutch influences but treated in a more vigorous and elaborate manner. The claw-and-ball foot became even more prominent and was subjected to many variations.

Claw and Ball Foot

The claw-and-ball originally held a deeply religious significance for the Chinese, with whom it typified the foot of the dragon, holding a pearl which had been obtained from the bottom of the sea.

Queen Anne furniture, no doubt, will remain popular in modern homes because of its simplicity, its livable charm and its wide adaptability.

LOUIS XIV (QUATORZE) PERIOD

1643 - 1715 FRANCE

IT IS not possible to more than mention the styles and the contemporaneous influences which flourished in France from 1643 to the latter part of the 18th Century.

It was a period fraught with romance, tremendous national influences, and powerful social movements. Louis XIV set an example in living and in art for the age that followed his death; which, as history shows, ascended and declined and eventually led to the French revolution and the execution of the nobility and aristocrats.

Louis XIV
Square Chair Leg

The period of Louis XIV, "the Grand" or "the Magnificent," was the most brilliant reign of any European King and the most important of any French king. He dominated art-expression as he dominated everything. He established royal work shops for the furtherance of his ideas; and due largely to his efforts, France at this time became the leading nation of Europe.

The best craftsmen worked for the glory of France regardless of their nationality. The style developed was regal and magnificent. While England was being oppressed with religious strife, France, though the Edict of Nantes, called to itself the Huguenots from Flanders and Holland; and these seekers for religious toleration included all kinds of craftsmen. Respect for art, commerce and science had been established by Cardinals Mazarin, Richelieu and others; and the Court developed the fashions created by its greatest artists and most skilled workmen.

Although Louis XIV was an absolute monarch, one who made himself the church and the state, his power was enlarged by his three successive mistresses: LaValliere, Madame de Montespan and Madame de Maintenon, who influenced and actually advanced the art of the period.

*Louis XIV
Cabriole*

The style of Louis XIV was broad and magnificent, with many straight lines and comparatively few curves. It was severe, classical, symmetrical; decorated beautifully, but not to excess; built for grandeur rather than for comfortable use. The ornament was always large in scale and alike on both sides, or bi-symmetrical. The shell usually was prominent.

The furniture expressed two opposed ideas. While the structure was formal and rectangular, it was decorated with motifs playfully informal, and the color combinations brought out the great display so loved by this monarch. Some of the legs of the furniture were straight, while others were cabriole in shape. The four legs of a chair were always alike. The feet were paws, cloven hoofs or carved acanthus leaves. The backs of the chairs were among the distinguishing features of the style. They were generally high and straight at the sides, and often straight

Century reproduction of Louis Quatorze Fauteuil
upholstered in Aubusson tapestry—a delightful
example of the period.

Two beautiful chairs of the period of Louis XIV of
France—faithful in construction and motif. They are
upholstered in needlework.

Louis XIV Arm Chair—Typical high straight-lined back, with characteristic legs and X-shaped stretchers of the period.

across the top. X-shape stretchers also were distinctive of this style.

In this period new types of decorations such as carving, painting, gilding, inlaying, lacquer-work and metal mounts were begun. Oak, walnut, ebony and chestnut were used extensively, with various rare woods for inlays. Marble was frequently employed for the tops of tables. The upholstery was exceedingly rich. The gorgeous tapestry of the Gobelin factory, Lyons velvets and damasks were used. It was prior to this time that James I of England, in order to keep pace with the country across the channel, imported Flemish weavers and caused to come into existence the Mortlake factory, also renowned for its remarkable fabrics.

The Louis Quatorze style is popular today although it must be modified for the modern home. It is suitable wherever dignity, formal and luxurious effects are desired. This furniture was originally at home in magnificent interiors, where entertaining was conducted on a large scale.

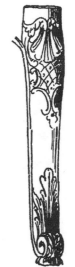

Cabriole Leg and Scroll Foot

Andre-Charles Boulle, born in 1642, was the outstanding furniture artist and designer during the reign of Louis XIV. He worked diligently through a long life, being still active in his eightieth year. He and his four sons left masterpieces of inlay, intricate and exquisite in conception and workmanship; and in this field they stand unsurpassed. He used tortoise shell extensively as a veneer into which he set his metal inlay; and the name "Boulle Work" is applied to this famous decorative process.

LOUIS XV (QUINZE)
PERIOD
1715 - 1774 FRANCE

Rococo Shell

LOUIS XV was the great-grandson of Louis XIV. When the old Louis died, after an unparalleled reign, the new king was only 5 years old. Until 1723, therefore, the Duke of Orleans governed as Regent; and the Regency period is properly considered a subdivision of the general Louis XV period. Louis XIV had instituted a tax system that exhausted the resources of the people. His great love of the gorgeous and his ponderous displays depleted the treasury. The Regent, accepting matters as he found them, squandered with a prodigal hand and helped pave the way for the unlucky heritage of Louis XVI.

The dissatisfaction of the people at this time at being over-taxed and imposed upon by an over-extravagant nobility, did not manifest itself in concerted action for nearly a hundred years; but the reign that followed made the French revolution almost a foregone conclusion.

Louis XV was ill-fitted to manage the affairs of a nation grown so great as France. Like the Duke of Orleans, he was licentious, extravagant and profligate. He surrounded himself with a weak, spineless and immoral court, the depravity

Three representative chairs of the Louis Quinze Period. Notice the entire absence of straight lines. These chairs are replicas by Century. The pattern at the right is known as the Slipper Chair.

Splendid reproduction of a Louis Quinze bergere.
The details of this piece are beautifully rendered.

of which is familiar to all students of history. He subjected himself to the influences of a succession of mistresses; two of whom, Madame du Barry and Madame de Pompadour, dominated state affairs during their ascendancy. The king professed an ultra-religious and virtuous nature, whereas he was quite the contrary. He instigated a tax system more severe than that of his great-grandfather. Hypocrisy was rampant. The age was one of sensuous pleasure and self-gratification.

And yet the art of the time is worthy of extended notice. The age was not a vulgar one. Vice and immorality, licentiousness and hypocrisy, were clothed in cloaks of refinement and gentility.

Louis XV Cabriole

During the Regency there was a lack of extremes in formalism and over-decoration; but as the popular French scroll and rococo motifs became more apparent, there took place a definite departure from the box-like and rectangular structures of Louis XIV.

Under the reign of Louis XV, the arts were generously patronized, and the encouragement of artists and craftsmen by promise of kingly rewards was continued. Impelled by assurances of high favor and position, they gave the best of their magnificent artistic ability to please the fancies of the king or king's mistresses.

There was a demand for softness and ease; and the designers of the day created furniture that for sheer beauty and charm has never been surpassed. Therefore the period developed structures of sinuous curves and contours. There were no straight lines; and the flowing lines became delicate and refined. No classic motifs were found. Ornament was always non-bi-symmetric — on the face of it beautiful, perhaps, but indicating lack of stability. The style eventually over-emphasized ormolu decoration; and rococo motifs predominated.

Madame de Pompadour greatly affected the art of the time and added to an already effeminate court lavish ideas of sensuous and sinuous grace. Characteristic details of the style were often expressed in an artistic combination of the rock and shell motifs, generally known as rococo. However, the endive leaf, the shell ornament, and the twisted forms imparted a large and sumptuous effect; and while flamboyant, were quite beautiful to the eye.

Louis XV furniture invariably possesses the cabriole leg, which takes rank as a distinctive characteristic of the style. The feet were the scroll-leaf while the dolphin-head sometimes was used. Arms of chairs and settees were short and flaring, with sharply curved supports; while the backs were broad with the framing ornately carved. They were usually upholstered, as were the seats. Underbracing, which had been X-shaped in the previous reign, disappeared in this period. In ornamentation, beauty dominated everything else. Plain surfaces were avoided. Moldings were lighter in effect. Panels were longer and not so square.

French Foot

The types of decoration used were carving, inlaying, painting, gilding and elaborate metal

Louis XV Table of carved walnut with skyros marble top.

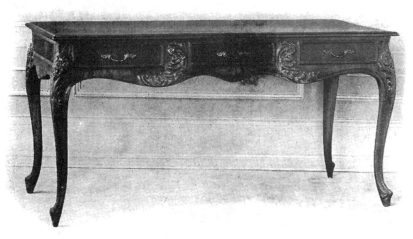

Louis Quinze Table of mahogany, with top and drawer fronts of rosewood. The cabriole legs and carved frame, with carved ornament, are typical.

Reproduction of a Chaise Longue of the Louis XV Period, typical of the style. The frames of Louis XV furniture often were painted or gilded to add to the decorative effect.

Reproduction of Louis XV Bergere, Tabouret and Smaller Bergere to form a Chaise Longue. The chaise longue always has been a popular piece of French furniture.

mounts.   Wreaths, flowers, lozenges, human figures and shells comprised the major motifs. Mahogany, walnut and ebony were much used but various rare woods were employed for inlay work.   The colors were very light and gay, the more popular being white and gold, pearl-gray, silver, rose, light greens and delicate blues.

Modern usage has disregarded completely the excessively rococo style of Louis XV furniture, but on the whole it has been adapted to many modern types of furniture.   Where a rich and sumptuous effect is desired, furniture of this period will provide it.

French Cabriole

LOUIS XVI (SEIZE) PERIOD
1774 - 1793 FRANCE

DURING the reign of Louis XV, the Queen Anne style was gaining popularity in England. Chippendale, Hepplewhite and the Adam Brothers were becoming prominent as designers, and the influence of the French Court was reflected in their designing. America was going through the development of national consciousness. Colonial governments were being formed, and the preparation for national independence was being made.

The grave responsibilities of guiding a nation headed for revolution fell upon the weak shoulders of Louis XVI, a young man wholly unfitted for the task. The people, smothered by the abandonment of everything for pleasure, cried out for a change. The pendulum was due to swing from the excesses of the former court to a saner era.

Swag

Louis XVI, low in mentality and taste, lacking initiative and character, was even too ambitionless to be immoral. He married Marie Antoinette of Austria, a child of 15, simple, gay, impulsive, refined and beautiful.

She came from the classic and strict environment of the Vienna court to the vice-ridden court of Versailles. As a matter of history, although Marie Antoinette brought with her an

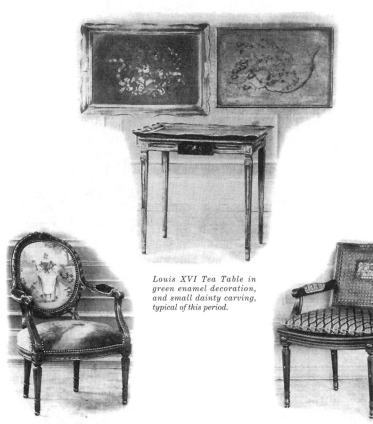

Louis XVI Tea Table in green enamel decoration, and small dainty carving, typical of this period.

Reproduction of a Louis Seize Fauteuil, classic in its simplicity. The legs are straight, tapered and grooved.

Fauteuil of walnut, with caned back and marquetry panel. The padded arms are typically French.

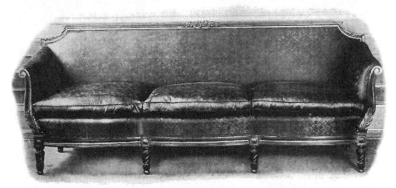

Louis Seize Sofa, with typical carved decorations on a mahogany frame.

Louis XVI Poudriere—The box is finished in crackled old bisquet enamel, with black and gold stripings, decorated in color. The stand is black lacquer decorated in green.

Louis XVI Sofa End Cabinet of walnut, with painted decorations and ormolu mounts. The top is black glass.

Reproduction of Louis Seize Bergere.

Reproduction of an exquisite Louis XVI Arm Chair. The classic motifs of the period are apparent.

appreciation of classic purity and a fine conception in matters of art, she did little to alleviate the sufferings or the feelings of her adopted country. Her sympathies were with Austria, at that time an enemy of France. She was extravagant, frequently tactless and irresponsible; but she was child-like in her innocence of the wanton excesses of her court, and she possessed the heritage of a people who were classicists.

The artists and craftsmen of the day were quick to bend their energies to please the Dauphiness; and never did there ensue so quick and so radical a change in furniture styles. The style of Louis XV and the style of Louis XVI stand for ideals as widely separated as were the styles themselves. They went almost from one extreme to the other.

Added impetus toward the classic ideals was given by the excavation and researches at Herculaneum and Pompeii. The unearthing of ancient treasures created a profound impression upon all thought during the middle of the Eighteenth Century, and the influence was felt in all parts of Europe, as shall be seen in reviewing the work of the Georgian designers of England.

Louis XVI
Scroll

The chief cabinet maker of the period was Riesener. He designed for Marie Antoinette for a score of years, but the ruling spirits of the Louis XVI style were Rousseau and Dugourc; although there were nearly a hundred other designers of ability during this time.

Structure at once changed from curved lines

and the cabriole leg to the straight line; from the non-bi-symmetric ornament to the bi-symmetrical. Architectural details in furniture became more minute and refined with the return of classic motifs and feeling. The style was more homelike. The general effect was dainty, graceful and elegant. Where curves were employed, they were long and slender.

The legs were a characteristic of the period—straight and tapered, usually fluted, and sometimes carved. Arms of chairs and sofas were straight or only slightly curved, being continuations of the front legs, either upright or curved slightly backward. Arm rests were padded. Underbracing was not used, nor would it have been in keeping with the general dainty effect.

*Louis XVI
Panel*

Marie Antoinette added garlands, love-birds, wreaths, baskets of flowers, rope carvings, pendant husks and pretty naturalistic things in adundance. The rosette became a dominating decoration. Festoons of ribbons, flaming torches, fluted columns, lyres and urns were prominent. The mounts were simpler than in preceding periods. Colors were soft and subdued. Light tints prevailed; and the favored color combinations were white and yellow, and white and green and gold. Mahogany was the favored wood. Walnut and satinwood also were used.

The Louis XVI style is a favorite one with modern designers. It adapts itself well to modern requirements; and, built along a simpler and smaller scale, is especially effective for bedroom furniture.

Louis XVI walnut and rosewood commode with ormolu mounts. The oval panel is inlaid with various colored woods. The top is Jaspe Oriental marble. The mirror frame is carved and gilded wood.

Louis XVI dressing table of walnut and rosewood enriched with ormolu mountings. The top is plate glass under which is displayed fine lace or other fabric. The chair is pure Louis XVI design.

This carved and partially gilt walnut bed with head and foot boards upholstered in silk damask is typical of the delicate and feminine influence apparent in furniture of the Louis XVI period.

The English contemporaries of this French period who produced for posterity were the Adam Brothers, Sheraton, Hepplewhite and other designers of the Late Georgian period. This was practically the close of the brilliant Golden Age of English furniture, as indeed, it had been a Golden Age of French accomplishment, an era that finally ended in the bloody revolution and the beheading of Louis Seize and his Queen.

*Louis XVI
Ram's Head*

In America the Colonies had gained independence from England and were setting up a new nation. The aid of Lafayette had turned the sentiment of new America toward France, and thus followed an influencing of Colonial forms of furniture by French ideas.

FRENCH EMPIRE
1795 - 1830

AFTER the execution of Louis XVI and the "Reign of Terror" which overthrew the Aristocracy, the Directory conducted the affairs of France until 1799 when Napoleon Bonaparte was made Consul. He became Emperor in 1804.

Griffin

The style in furniture that followed was not a development. Napoleon, feeding his vanity, directed that a new style replace the delicate, ornamental and effeminate patterns of Marie Antoinette's choosing. It was almost a royal edict, a command. Napoleon, of course, was militaristic. He loved pomp and show; but this new style found ready acceptance by the French people, who were anxious to be rid of all reminders of the nobility. In fact, any style other than those which had been in vogue for nearly 200 years would have been acceptable.

Napoleon's Egyptian campaign had much to do with the trend that was to follow. Napoleon favored the pomp and glory of ancient Rome, and he surrounded himself with classic forms and insignia of that time. Artists were commissioned to carry out these ideas. To flatter the Emperor, they brought forth in their furniture productions much of "the glory that was Greece and the grandeur that was Rome."

Directoire chair typical of the style.

Empire Pier Glass in mahogany with ormolu mounts. Note the Egyptian and classic motifs.

Imperial Roman type of arm chair decreed by Napoleon—The top rail is scrolled backward in the manner of the Greek style.

*The throne of Napoleon—an excellent
example of the Empire style.*

As a result, the furniture of this period was artificial. It did not reflect a natural sentiment or growth. It was the least French of any French style. Its imitation of ancient forms resulted in a pompous and grandiose style that was quite in keeping with the vanity of the "Little Corporal." Still, its influence was felt in various parts of Europe and spread rapidly to America, resulting here in what is known as American Empire.

The general effect of French Empire furniture was imparted by plain surfaces with brass mounts of antique emblems. Lines were mostly straight with a few simple curves. Legs were straight and turned, or slightly curved. Metal feet were much used. Paw and claw feet, showing the classic influence, were employed frequently. The moldings were heavy and imposing, while the ornaments were usually metal mounts, columns and scroll supports; although some painting and gilding was used.

Winged Griffin

Among the motifs of this style were symbolic designs of conquest, such as the sword, shield, winged human figures and imperial animals, such as the lion and the eagle; while the Egyptian sphinx, the outspread-wings and flying-disk, so common in Egyptian art, cornucopias, the lyre, acanthus leaves, flaming torches, the Greek band, the pineapple (a symbol of equality and hospitality), Greek honeysuckle and laurel wreaths enclosing the Napoleonic letter "N" easily identify this period. The star, representing the conqueror, and the motif known as "Napoleon bees" were found scattered through the style. The bees are said to be emblematic of the enterprise and activity of the Napoleonic era.

The upholstery of the Empire period was rich and heavy. The colors were deep green, red, royal blue and purple.

Mahogany was the chief wood, but rosewood and ebony also were used.

In recent years, the Empire style has been more or less revived through a renewed interest in one of America's early designers, Duncan Phyfe; and thus it has its place in the modern scheme of living.

Honeysuckle

CHIPPENDALE

1705 - 1779

THOMAS CHIPPENDALE, the great designer, was born shortly after Queen Anne ascended to the English throne. Ten years later Louis XIV of France died. Chippendale was the son of a wood carver and cabinetmaker of repute, of Worcester, England. He inherited his artistic ability and his love of fine furniture. It is not at all surprising that he should have been influenced by the increasing attention to the home, and the desire for better and more complete furnishings. Nor is it odd that he was inspired, to a certain extent, by the artistic output during the time of the French monarch, Louis XV.

Ribband Back

Chippendale was the first cabinetmaker to attach his name to a style. He was a master designer, a peerless carver, and a remarkable craftsman. He was particularly adept at choosing ideas from other periods and other countries. He even adapted Oriental motifs, until he evolved what has become known as Chinese-Chippendale. Even the Gothic supplied him with inspirations. But always did Chippendale impart to the styles something of himself that stamped them with individuality, made them harmonious, and above all, made them English. He was a good business man and a good sales-

Foliated Knee

Ladder Back

man. In 1754 he wrote and published the first book on furniture designs; and, in so doing, he identified individual designs with the maker's name.

The style is richly carved in mahogany, with a free use of curves gracefully, beautifully and substantially proportioned. It may be more difficult to recognize than the average, for the reason that Chippendale was influenced by definite styles himself. But generally speaking, substantial beauty, with marvelous carving, no matter what the style, is identical with Chippendale.

Perhaps the claw-and-ball foot is one of the most characteristic motifs. The foot was used with cabriole legs; but other feet used with cabriole legs were the club, web, scroll, paw, dolphin, leaf and slipper. Although the cabriole leg was used by Chippendale to a great extent, the straight leg was employed on his Gothic and Chinese styles. The arms of his chairs were curved and flaring at the end, and usually joined the uprights at an angle; while the supports were shaped forward, at the side rails of the seat. This feature is a definite Chippendale characteristic.

The backs of Chippendale chairs always have been noted for their beauty and conformation to the styles he followed; yet they are approximately all the same in proportion. They were inclined to be square in outline, with serpentine-shaped tops. The hoop-shaped tops, together with the curved uprights of the Queen Anne period, were not employed by Chippendale.

Chinese-Chippendale Chair—A Century adaptation, which illustrates the versatility of the great Georgian designer in choosing foreign styles for his own use.

Reproduction of a Chippendale chair, American, about 1760-70. It is mahogany. Original now in the Metropolitan Museum of Art.

Reproduction of Chippendale Knee-Hole Desk of Cuban Mahogany.

Reproduction of a Chippendale carved mahogany arm chair.

Reproduction of a carved mahogany Chippendale chair of the last half of the 18th Century.

Chippendale sofa of carved mahogany. Note how the pierced stretchers give a lightness to the substantial understructure of the frame.

In the later Georgian one finds the uprights straight. The backs were broad and flat but occasionally "dipped" or "spooned" when they were not upholstered. The well known "ladderback" is so-called because of a number of horizontal bars between the uprights, and the fretback is a back filled with fret work. The ribbon, or ribband, back had a carved splat consisting of loops of ribbon; while the splat-back is identified by the piercing or interlacing of various designs in the splat. Chippendale's Chinese fret-work patterns and padded-back chairs had square backs. All the backs of Chippendale chairs were quite fanciful, and they remain as one of the high-lights of his style.

This designer was free in his use of various motifs. Scrolls, acanthus leaves, knotted ribbons and interlaced straps were favorites. French ornamentation, such as the rococo shells and extravagant curves, was employed. The "C" scroll was an almost inevitable Chippendale detail. Lion heads and masks of the Georgian times were used.

Pierced Splat

As has been said, mahogany was the material chosen for Chippendale's exquisite carving. And he was fastidious in his choice of mahogany. Walnut was employed sparingly. He made practically all types of furniture. Sideboards, as understood in the modern home, came into use; and for the first time bookcases became an important consideration.

Chippendale always will be a source of inspiration for modern designers, who ever have drawn upon his vast store-house for ideas. Chippendale's furniture not only looked sound, but actually was structurally sound; and much of it has remained to the present day in a perfect state of preservation. Galleries and museums where it is exhibited provide a Mecca for those who wish to study and learn from this designer's contributions to posterity.

Chippendale died in 1779. His influence had been paramount for thirty years and his work even improved in his latter years.

Dolphin Foot

HEPPLEWHITE
INFLUENCE 1770-1790

ENGLAND, by this time, was well upon the threshold of the last quarter of the 18th Century. This period is known as the "Golden Age of Furniture." It is made outstandingly remarkable, not only by the work that Chippendale left to succeeding generations, but by the presence of that great contemporaneous group— Hepplewhite, the Brothers Adam and Sheraton.

In 1774, Louis XV of France died, and with his passing also passed the overdone rococo style of that nation. At the time the Hepplewhite style prevailed in England, the classic Louis XVI ideals were popular in France. This antique style tendency not only was promoted, but was definitely influenced by the unearthing of the ruins of Pompeii about this time.

Ears of Wheat

George Hepplewhite was a London cabinetmaker and an original designer. He developed an individual style which attained a great popularity, and his influence was widespread. The high points of the Hepplewhite style are lightness, gracefulness and elegance, with emphasis on the pure beauty of line. His work was refined, free from bizarre motifs, and showed a great deal of the Louis XVI influence, a type he not only adapted, but frequently copied. In spite of the slender characteristics of the style, he achieved sturdy English structural qualities.

Hepplewhite may be distinguished from other light furniture of the day by the graceful straight leg forms, the serpentine fronts (which, however, always were a convex or swelling out curve), and concave, cut-in corners. Wheat-ears, Prince of Wales feathers and bell-flower husks were much used for ornamentation. On the chairs one usually finds shield-shaped backs (this shape being extensively used also for mirrors), and the unusual short, curved arms. Curves emphasize the Hepplewhite style, but always they were refined.

Shield Back

Legs, however, were usually straight—the cabriole leg having passed out with Chippendale and Louis XV, as far as England and France were concerned. They often were square and tapered, terminating in a spade-foot. The tapered, round leg also was used. Often it was reeded or grooved, and sometimes carved with an intertwining spiral band. The spade-foot was a favorite Hepplewhite detail.

Hepplewhite, however, was famous for his chairs. Although all of his pieces bore rare distinction, many claim that his greatest originality was displayed in those structures. The shield-shaped chair-back was the most distinctive; but this was modified by the hoop back, the interlacing heart back and the oval back. A point to remember is that the backs of Hepplewhite chairs were supported by a rail above the seat, which joined the slender curved continuations of the back legs.

*Hepplewhite Desk made of antique fiddle-back
maple with green panels illuminated with
painted floral motifs.*

*A Hepplewhite Sofa, designed in the
French taste.*

*Arm chair of mahogany in the style of
Hepplewhite, American, about 1785-95.*

*A typical Hepplewhite design, characteristic in every detail—
interlacing hearts, the light, airy effect, the arms joining the
back from the side, straight, reeded tapered legs with spade feet,
and upholstery brought down over all the frame.*

Circular Front Commode of curly maple with satinwood panels. Painted foliage and floral decorations, with green striping embellish the surface. The hexagon medallion bears a portrait of Fanny Kemble as "Julia" after the manner of Thomas Sully, a noted painter of the Eighteenth Century.

The shape of the mirror frame with its indentures and classic top ornament was greatly favored during the time of Hepplewhite.

An Eighteenth Century English Seat in the Hepplewhite manner, typical of the classic revival of that period.

Semi-circular Commode, veneered with harewood and satinwood. The roses inlaid on the oral panel are naturalistic in treatment. Typical of the Hepplewhite-Adam school.

Typical Hepplewhite chair of carved mahogany.

Reproduction of a Hepplewhite chair of prima vera and satinwood with painted decorations.

Reproduction of an 18th Century Arm Chair of mahogany.

Hepplewhite Arm Chair in the French taste—It is noted that Hepplewhite's French furniture—a style he greatly admired, is the most esteemed of all his works.

The designs popular with Hepplewhite were the lyre, the honeysuckle, the urn, "S" curves and Prince of Wales feathers. The seats were frequently rounded at the back; but others were square and tapering. Usually they were upholstered, and this upholstering generally was brought down over the frame all around.

Although mahogany was a favorite wood, Hepplewhite employed also rosewood, satinwood, tulipwood, harewood and other rare selections. Painting was the favorite decoration. Carving, light and classic in its feeling, however, was not infrequently used.

*Prince of Wales
Feathers*

Hepplewhite published a book on furniture design which proved to be a valuable addition to the literature of cabinetmaking. He established his own company about the middle of the 18th Century and some twenty-five years later he had won his reputation. The Prince of Wales was a patron of Hepplewhite & Co., and this recognition by the royalty also added to the popularity of his furniture. At the time of his death in 1786, his productions were widely sought.

The Hepplewhite style meets the modern demand for furniture of light and graceful forms. It is not necessary to modify or make great changes from the original models; and in well appointed homes, usually one or more pieces distinctly Hepplewhite, are to be found.

ADAM BROTHERS
LATER 18TH CENTURY

ROBERT and James Adam, contemporaries of Hepplewhite and Sheraton, impressed themselves upon English architecture and art during the later part of the 18th Century. Originally, they were not furniture designers. They were sons of a Scotch architect and were associated in the practice of architecture. They not only designed homes, but also were designers and decorators of interiors.

Husk

The demand upon them for furniture to harmonize with their matchless interiors practically forced them into furniture designing; and although they were not actual builders their conceptions of furniture are models of classic interpretation. And their styles proved a most important influence; although originally the brothers had little intention of doing more than filling their commissions properly and finishing artistically the houses they had designed.

Robert Adam had spent several years studying architecture in Italy. Greatly influenced by classic art, he became one of the greatest authorities in England on this style of design. Then, too, the discovery of the ruins of Pompeii renewed an active interest in classic design, just as the unearthing of the tomb of King Tut-ankh-amen created general interest and influenced styles in our own modern times.

This chair is late Eighteenth Century. It is in maple with a satinwood finish. The influence of the Brothers Adam is apparent both in construction and motif detail.

An Eighteenth Century type humidor in maple with panels of satinwood. The small box superimposed on the onyx top contains an electric lighter.

An Eighteenth Century drop leaf table. The decorations are characteristic of the era, while the contour of the piece reflects the classic.

A group of Chairs of the Adam Style—The upper left shows the Prince of Wales feathers so much used by Hepplewhite. The lower left is the typical Adam square back—low seat square and tapered, legs tapered and fluted. Characteristic arms. The classic lyre ornament was greatly favored.

The Adam Brothers' interpretation of the classic introduced forms and motifs quite different from any that had been used prior to that time. It is true that sometimes they designed furniture that was structurally impractical; but the style always was slender, refined, straight-lined, inclined to flat surfaces, and adorned with well conceived classic ornamentation. There is little doubt that Hepplewhite in England and the designers in France who produced forms to meet the fancies of Marie Antoinette, received much inspiration from the Brothers Adam.

This furniture represents the attainment of a very fine ideal. It is quite natural that it should have remained popular in modern times. The cultured, graceful lines and elegant simplicity with which Adam furniture is endowed make it admirably suited for the well appointed home.

Adam
Square Foot

The style is distinguished by its dainty and delicate ornamentation, rather than by its symmetrical structure. The cabinet work was rectangular. Legs and feet were slender and small, being round and fluted with turned feet, or tapered with spade feet. Practically everything was light in effect. Moldings were narrow. Underbracing was used only occasionally. Carving in low relief was used sparingly. Inlay permitted the use of satinwood and other rare woods. Painting and gilding were popular, and some famous artists of the time, including Angelika Kauffmann, Cipriani, and Pergolesi, were employed to decorate various pieces.

The Adam style makes use of the classic lyre and the urn, or vase, which were originally religious ornaments of antiquity. Small round or oval shapes, with fan-like disks, frequently enclosed, were characteristic. Draped classic figures, swag floral pendants, husks, fruits, rams' heads, and purely Greek motifs, such as the egg-and-dart molding, the acanthus leaf and anthemion also were drawn upon liberally.

Urn

Obviously, a refined type of upholstery to match this elegant style was necessary; and in Adam furniture one finds delicate French brocades much used. Mahogany was the popular wood in use, particularly for carved pieces; although various cheaper woods, which were painted or gilded, were employed.

SHERATON
1750 - 1806

THOMAS SHERATON was the last great designer of the 18th Century. He has been called the greatest of the English designers and cabinetmakers of this "Golden Age of Furniture." Also he has been called the "English Louis XVI"; because his style was imbued with classic principles of outline and ornamentation that characterized the French designs.

Spade Foot

Sheraton had been preceded by Chippendale and his influence came a little later than Hepplewhite and the Adam Brothers. In fact, he was able to profit by and learn from the works of these masters. During his life, America gained her independence and the French Revolution developed. In spite of these conflicts, however, his furniture remained chaste and pure. It betrayed no influence of the war-like times.

Chippendale, Hepplewhite, and Robert and James Adam were successful business men. They had money and lived in a manner befitting their tastes. Sheraton, on the other hand, found his life a continual struggle to provide the bare necessities for his family. A genius of the greatest versatility, he lacked the flair for money-making. In addition to being a designer and cabinetmaker, he was a drawing master, author, publisher, and preacher. Yet, in spite of his ability to do a great many things superlatively well, he lived in poverty, and died in disappointment.

Sheraton frankly adapted many of the Louis XVI styles, to which he contributed his own artistic knowledge and conceptions. The result, which is a prominent characteristic of all Sheraton furniture, was a subtle gracefulness, a remarkable appreciation of form and correct geometrical proportions. His work at all times shows classic dignity, refinement and restraint.

Oval Back

In looking at Sheraton furniture, one is impressed with the purity and beauty of perpendicular lines. He never designed short curves. Whenever he employed the curve at all, it became a graceful sweep.

Sheraton used the oval to a considerable extent; while the lyre, slender urns and latticework were characteristic. Reeding and fluting also marked the style. He used swags, the cockle-shell, the star, fan-shapes, and small ornamental disks. Inlay was a favored decoration and he worked in many beautiful woods. Turning, veneering and painting were used. The carving was delicate and light.

Sheraton knew construction. Although his furniture was light in character, it was structurally sound. The legs were exceedingly slender and were usually round, tapered and reeded. Another type was the square and tapered; while during the latter part of his career, some of the table legs were spiral-turned, the acanthus leaf being used. The feet are not conspicuous. He used the spade-foot, as did Hepplewhite, the

Banner Screen of the 18th Century in old ivory with green decorations.

Reproduction of an Eighteenth Century Arm Chair, in the manner of Sheraton. It is painted and decorated with floral designs and medallions.

Sheraton—Reproduction of a painted arm chair of maple with characteristic decorations in color. The low back with its geometrical ornament is typical of this designer.

Reproduction of a Sheraton Arm Chair, the original of which is in the collection of A. T. Pope of Hillstead, Farmington, Conn.

Eighteenth Century Table of mahogany, with beautiful harmonies of thuya, burl rosewood, vermilion, tulip wood and crotch mahogany. Sheraton was a master in his employment of rare wood for inlays.

Sheraton Arm Chair—Note the slender arms and the reeded legs—typical details of construction and ornamentation.

Sheraton Chair—The back is characteristic.

Tilt Table with pie-crust edge, of Sheraton design. The top is crotch mahogany with a panel of zebra wood inlaid with various woods in a floral design.

Reproduction of a Sheraton Easy Chair.

block-foot and occasionally the French foot, which curved slightly outward.

The most typical Sheraton chair-back was square, with a central panel rising slightly above the top rail. The lower rail usually kept the back well up from the seat. The arms were quite characteristic. They started high on the up-rights of the chair and swept downward in a very extended "S" shape to the supports, which frequently were a continuation of the front legs.

The Hepplewhite and Sheraton styles are very similar; in fact, without study, it is difficult to tell them apart. Sheraton, however, used more underbracing than Hepplewhite, often employ-ing the X-shape stretcher. This, however, was seldom used on chairs. Hepplewhite pulled his seat-cover well over the apron; while Sheraton permitted a part of the seat frame to show.

Dip Seat

Mahogany was favored, but Sheraton was a master at assembling various woods. Satinwood, tulipwood, sycamore, and rosewood for inlays, were used with discrimination. The period fre-quently is referred to as "The Age of Satinwood."

Before Sheraton died in 1806, the French Empire style had begun to sweep over Europe. Sheraton, always had looked to France and classic sources for his inspirations. In an effort to appeal to the popular taste, he tried to fashion furniture after the manner of the Empire styles. In this he was a signal failure; and that period of his work was least worthy of his career.

Sheraton possessed a too great self-esteem and an unfortunate personality. He never hesitated to point out the merits of his own designs, nor to belittle those of many of his contemporaries. As a result, he was disliked, nor was there a disposition on the part of those with whom he came in contact to excuse his egotism because of his rare genius.

But none of this has been reflected in his furniture, which remains highly esteemed. The artistic merit of Sheraton design is felt everywhere today. It is admirably suited for modern use and always imparts refinement to the home.

Medallion

OTHER DESIGNERS OF THE GEORGIAN PERIOD

ONE hears so much of the Great Quartette of furniture designers of the 18th Century that one is prone to overlook the existence of other designers of the wonderful Georgian era. There were others, however, who contributed much to the artistic development of the age.

It is true they were the lesser lights, men who never achieved the recognition or fame of their more successful contemporaries; but many of their original conceptions were chosen and amplified by the greater men.

Broken Pediment with Finial

In many cases, the best work produced by these "lesser lights" compares well with the work of those of greater fame; but on the whole, they did not maintain the standard of general excellence established by these men, and some of their articles were very bad. Nevertheless, they left an impression on English furniture in their day and should be mentioned in a review of this character.

Thomas Shearer leads this group of secondary names, which includes Sir William Chambers, Ince and Mayhew, and R. Manwaring, Copeland, Lock, Johnson, Crunden and the Gillows.

Paw Foot

Sir William Chambers spent a part of his early manhood in China. So impressed was he

Lion Knee

with the architecture and art of the country that he made many sketches of the details and characteristics of the buildings, furniture and gardens. Upon his return to England he published a large folio containing various engravings of his impressions. The book was issued in 1757. In the meantime, Sir William had devoted himself wholly to the practice of architecture. Later he engaged in interior decoration.

Chambers it was, and not Chippendale, who introduced the vogue for Chinese art. Chippendale had access to Chambers' book and profited thereby. Chambers, no doubt, proved a source of inspiration for the Brothers Adam, for Hepplewhite and for Sheraton; for, although his name is connected with Chinese art, he was a classicist in design and ranked high as an architect, decorator and designer.

Ince and Mayhew were contemporaries of Chippendale and attempted to produce furniture in the manner of Chippendale. They fell far short in their copying, however, of even Chippendale's less-inspired productions. It is said they catered to the tastes of the day and produced designs in the Chinese, Gothic and French styles, displaying an inability to choose the good and avoid the bad.

Cabochon

R. Manwaring, another of the 18th Century designers who attempted to follow the trail blazed by Chippendale, has been frowned upon by writers on furniture subjects. His designs "were without grace, inspiration; banal and frumpishly respectable." Manwaring published the "Cabinet and Chairmaker's Real Friend

Georgian Arm Chair—Made of mahogany. The shell, scrolls, and pad feet were popular motifs of the time.

Georgian sofa in mahogany with cabriole legs and pad feet.

English upholstered chair and sofa with down cushion backs and seats. The wood bases are carved and gilded in the style of the Georgian period and the detail is representative of the time.

and Companion" in 1765. Another was published the following year. They are said to contain fantastic atrocities, which "if they were ever executed have happily not survived." Nevertheless, Manwaring seems to have been the originator of the fretted bracket between the legs and seat-rail of chairs—an item of design adapted by Chippendale and frequently used with good effect.

Thomas Shearer was a contemporary of Sheraton and Hepplewhite and a co-worker with the latter. His work entitles him to more respect and admiration than can be accorded to the other "lesser lights" of the Georgian period.

Shearer's work was similar to that of Hepplewhite and Sheraton. In fact, the general characteristics are so similar that a review of Shearer details would, in a sense, be repetition.

Claw and Ball

It was Shearer, however, who first developed the distinctive type of sideboard that since has become so identified with the designs of Hepplewhite and Sheraton. Before either of these greater designers had made beautifully inlaid sideboards, with serpentine fronts and tapered legs, Shearer had designed and produced examples of this type that compare favorably with anything produced later.

Shearer's pieces, however, did not possess the delicacy of line and grace of proportion found in Hepplewhite's or Sheraton's productions; and for this reason principally, his work suffers by comparison.

Satyr-Masque Knee

COLONIAL AMERICAN STYLES
1620 - 1795

ALTHOUGH any consideration of Colonial styles in America must take us back to the Early Jacobean in England and the time prior to the reign of Louis XIV in France, it is quite proper to consider the Colonial styles last. Indeed, America during its early days became a veritable melting pot for furniture, even as it has since proved a melting pot for mankind.

Claw and Ball Foot

There is no such thing as a definite Colonial style in the sense that one refers to the style of Chippendale, or the period of Louis XVI. It was, more correctly, a period during which many styles were used and fused—styles that were adapted to the needs of the colonists.

From the landing of the Pilgrims in 1620, each successive ship brought settlers who either had their own household furnishings with them, or possessed ideas of what such furnishings should be; and these ideas were those which had been gained in their own countries. Then, too, artisans from the old world made the old styles; for, while they sought a new world where they could worship according to the dictates of their own hearts, they remained British in thought and naturally designed and built their furnishings in the manner of the British school.

American Tilt Table with revolving pie-crust top of fiddle-back maple, decorated.

An Early American design. This chair is painted a soft old red with decoration in color. Rush bottom seat.

Reproduction of an Early Colonial Windsor type—the bow back. The original—a rare example—is from the collection of Ex-Congressman Hayes, of Lexington, Mass.

Windsor Chairs originated in England and were named after the town of Windsor. They were brought to America by early colonists, and while subjected to many variations, have remained popular ever since.

A New England Colonial chair of a rare design. The original is in Kittery, Maine.

Colonial Arm Chair of Sheraton design.

Colonial Arm Chair—Jacobean motif. Reproduction from the original owned by the Connecticut Historical Society in Hartford, Conn.

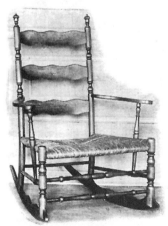

New England type of the American Arm Rocker of maple turned, slat back chair. Rocking chairs were an American invention.

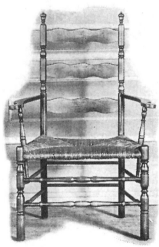

American Arm Chair with rush seat—The support for the short arms are spindles which extend through the seat rail to the upper stretchers—a characteristic feature.

Block-front Desk made for Brig. Gen. Huntington of Norwich, Conn., about 1765. This style of desk is closely associated with Early American furnishings, and the various types were named after well known men of the period. Now in the Metropolitan Museum of Art.

Chippendale style of Lowboy, similar to other Georgian pieces, and always popular in the Colonies.

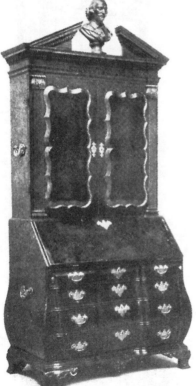

A Highboy with carved bust of Shakespeare serving as a finial between the members of a broken pediment. Photograph of original now in the Metropolitan Museum.

In Colonial furniture, therefore, one finds a mixture of practically all the English periods and many Dutch forms. France, too, contributed somewhat to the style trend in America, although her influence did not become paramount until after the French revolution.

The lives of the early American settlers were full of hardships. Their wants were basic. They had little time or thought for furniture that did not meet a strictly utilitarian need. We find therefore in the earlier days, Elizabethan and Jacobean styles which were popular in England at that time. These actually conformed to the needs of the earlier settlers. Later on, the William and Mary style in England crossed the ocean and supplied the colonists with furniture that also was suited to the somewhat improved standard of living.

Spooned Back

As America became more settled and life less vigorous, thoughts naturally turned to the betterment of the home. About this time the Queen Anne style predominated in England. It became popular in America, and so remained for many years.

One finds also the influence of the early Georgian period and Chippendale styles up to the time of the Revolution; and there was a Hepplewhite and Sheraton influence after the Revolution. At the time, the influence of these designers was felt to a lesser degree because, following the War of Independence, the American people possessed a strong aversion to everything English. Turning to France, largely out of a sense of gratitude for her assistance during the

Pie Crust Table

Revolution, early America adopted the styles of the French Empire. From the French Empire style, America evolved and developed a style of its own, which has become known as American Empire.

Colonial styles were plainer and often sturdier than the foreign models from which they were adapted. There were few complex or fanciful elements about them. There was, however, freedom of line, at once straightforward, durable and usable. Its simplicity is that element which today endows Colonial forms with quaint charm.

Splat

As has been said, the decoration of the furniture of Colonial times was typical of the different periods of English and other styles. Although the Colonists' interpretation of European styles tended to eliminate everything not necessary, hand-wrought mounts, drawer-pulls of iron or brass were used quite lavishly for decorative effects.

Although imported mahogany came into use in the early part of the 18th Century, native oak, pine, ash, hickory, gum, apple, pear, cherry and maple were used to make most of the furniture of the times. Native black-walnut also was popular. Reed and rush seats were in demand, but later, upholstery was employed.

Bracket Foot

Colonial furniture is deservedly popular in America today. For modern use it is somewhat lighter than original forms; but the style is charming, appeals because of its historical background, and is suited to modern requirements of beauty and usefulness.

*Small Easy Chair of maple.
Early American.*

*Chair of Early American design. Made
of antique maple, with upholstered seat.
About 1700.*

*Early American Sideboard in maple, the simplicity of
which is largely responsible for its charm.*

AMERICAN BARREL CHAIR

(Reproduction)

This chair is upholstered in Vauxhall linen. From 1750 to the early 'teens of the nineteenth century, Vauxhall Gardens was a popular and stylish resort of the social, literary, and artistic groups of London. The garden, with its quaint formal walks and Italian pavilions, forms the background of the linen design, while in the foreground are thirty-four distinguished Georgians.

Among these are the Prince of Wales, later George IV; Mrs. Sarah Siddons, actress; Horace Walpole, author; David Garrick, actor; Edward Gibbon, historian; Tobias George Smollett, novelist; Oliver Goldsmith, poet; William Hogarth, pictorial satirist; James Boswell, biographer; Dr. Samuel Johnson, literary arbiter and critic, and the famous painters Angelika Kauffmann, Thomas Gainsborough and Sir Joshua Reynolds.

American Cabinet of the first quarter of the 18th Century. Finished in Chinese raised lacquer on a blue-gold flaked ground, resembling lapis lazuli. The interior is painted a very soft green.

THE AMERICAN FEDERAL ERA
(WILLIAM SAVERY)
1760 - 1800

S OME years ago, in a brilliantly designed and splendidly built lowboy, was found the label of a little-known Philadelphia craftsman, William Savery. The collecting world was thrown into great excitement at the discovery of a new name in American furniture history worthy to rank with that of Phyfe. To Savery were attributed various other exquisite relics of the revolutionary period, and a close search was begun for other works of this master.

Broken Pediment

Research, however, has shown conclusively that Savery, who died in prosperous circumstances in 1787, at the age of 65, was but one of perhaps half-a-dozen able makers, who lived in Philadelphia, New York and New England, designing and thinking in terms of Chippendale and the later Georgian masters.

These men equaled and often even excelled the best work of the London shops. They found appreciative patronage in the wealthy merchants, landowners, and shipowners of the day. And, although the general manner was borrowed from the fashionable English designers, a certain nationalism began to appear in their work. The influence of Chippendale's earlier conceptions, for example, far outlasted in America its English vogue. And so are found many of his mannerisms

—the cabriole leg, claw and ball feet, hooded tops, broken pediments, finials, carved busts, shell and rococo motifs, and metal drawer pulls and lock plates, in combination with the later English manner of handling woods and panelling.

In general, it will be found in the furniture of this period that the woods (usually mahogany and satinwood, with curly maple and "balata", a mahogany substitute) are rather better chosen than in contemporary English furniture. Often, too, the pieces are rather more solidly constructed; chairs, for instance, quite often have the seat frame extending entirely through the rear posts, where it is pegged in place.

Serpent Foot

Almost every month, as this is written, is adding to the sum of knowledge regarding these marvelously skilled American makers. So well-defined is their manner that authorities are beginning to call their school the "Federal" school, in distinction from the less finished "Early American" which, of course, includes everything from the surviving Jacobean influence down to the last of the Queen Anne influence.

Pictured is the Savery label which did so much to teach this lesson on the early culture of the republic.

All Sorts of Chairs and Joiners Work Made and Sold by *William Savery* At the Sign of the Chair, a little below the Market, in Second Street. PHILADELPHIA.

William Savery—This is a photograph of the dressing table in which was found the Savery shop label referred to in the text.

American Colonial Highboy by William Savery, showing the Georgian influence in this country at that time. The original piece, of which this is a photograph, is in the Metropolitan Museum of Art.

Reproduction of an Early 19th Century Duncan Phyfe arm chair in mahogany. The original is in the Metropolitan Museum of Art.

A Duncan Phyfe American chair in mahogany.

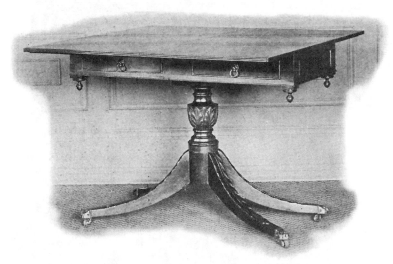

Duncan Phyfe. An American flip-top table of mahogany. The curved out legs are typical of the classic lines of Phyfe.

AMERICAN EMPIRE
1795 - 1830

MODERN manufacturers find a wealth of inspiration in early American forms; and many beautiful pieces have been built around motifs which predominated during the early years of this country as an independent nation. For the sake of proper classification, these styles are generally grouped under the head of Early American, and are not considered strictly Colonial styles.

The American Empire period, however, was distinctive. This was the vogue that sprung up after the War of Independence with England, and epitomized the dislike of the Colonists for things English. It was natural for America to turn to France. The style of the French Directoire period already was felt in this country, and when the Napoleonic regime dictated the fashions at the beginning of the 19th Century, America also, took to these pompous forms.

American Empire furniture resembles very much the French Empire period styles in that similar characteristics are found in each. Modifications were made by American designers, however, which is to their credit.

The motifs found in furniture decoration include acanthus leaves, the lyre, the pineapple, the cornucopia, winged-griffin feet, lion claws

Leaf and Feather Carving

and bear claws, quite as these same motifs are found in the French Empire styles. Furniture was carved and some of the carving was gilded. Metal-mounts were popular and scrolls were much in evidence. Heavy cornices were prominent.

The lines of this furniture were neither very good nor very bad. Curved and straight lines were used, although cabinet work was usually rectangular. Proportions were large and massive, and in effect very substantial. The legs were straight, or curved outward in the classic style of the curule, which later was identified with the works of Duncan Phyfe. The feet were continuations of legs, in some instances; but the French influence, as shown in the feet and claws of animals, together with the scroll, the bracket and turned feet, still prevailed.

Cornucopia Motif with Paw Foot

Arms of chairs began well up on the uprights of the back, swept downward in a fairly graceful curve, and terminated in a scroll. Sofa-arms were usually rolled over. The backs of chairs were low and simple in design, while the top rail was usually curved to fit the contour of the body, a detail typically Greek. Mahogany was used almost to the exclusion of everything else.

It was at this time that the "sleigh" beds came into fashion, and it was from these that the present style of bed was evolved. Four-poster beds without canopies, however, were still being made. These were designed with both high and short posts and frequently were quite heavy and elaborately carved. The pineapple top and the acanthus leaf were favorite motifs. Sideboards

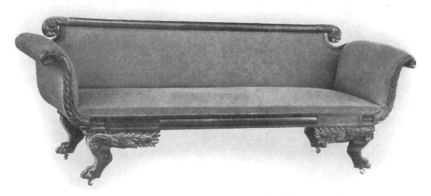

*American Empire—Post Colonial Period
reproduction. original was owned by the
Washington family.*

*Reproduction of an Early American sofa
of the Post Colonial Period. Empire motifs
are apparent.*

American Chairs of the 19th Century made of maple and mahogany. The upper two chairs have painted decorations.

Nineteenth Century Corner Cupboard of mahogany with crotch mahogany panels. The upper part is papered in an old New England design.

were prominent in the furnishings of the time, and center tables came into vogue. Chairs were lighter and more graceful. Upholstered sofas were popular.

The four-poster bed served a strictly utilitarian purpose in this country as it did in England. Homes were rudely built, or poorly heated; and the canopies and curtains of the four-poster beds were designed for the purpose of keeping the occupants warm. But as time went on, houses were better made and these unsanitary accessories were dropped.

Stenciled furniture and furniture with hand painted designs became popular in about 1820. The fact that young women of the day studied painting, just as they studied literature and music, promoted this vogue. After they were married and had their own homes, it was quite the fashion to decorate furniture, china and other articles about the house.

Stencil

DUNCAN PHYFE

1795 - 1847

D UNCAN PHYFE was America's first furniture designer of prominence; and it is maintained by many that his designs have not been surpassed since. America owes a great deal to this artist for having saved this country from the more or less debasing influences of the French Empire styles. He was apparently the only American to develop a distinctive style of his own. Like other great designers, he chose from whatever sources he desired and adapted his findings to his own uses, always making some modification of his own creations that gave to them an individuality.

Lyre Back

But just as Sheraton was lead astray in an attempt to fashion furniture after the style of the French Empire, so did Duncan Phyfe fail in his attempt to make anything beautiful from the atrocities of the Victorian era that became the vogue near the close of his career.

Phyfe was born in Scotland. He came to this country in 1783. Eventually he established a shop at 35 Partition Street (now Fulton) in New York. Here during the height of his career he employed more than 100 workmen, and it is said that this pioneer artist and craftsman did more to educate American taste than any of the English cabinetmakers. His work extended over

Reproduction of Duncan Phyfe drop leaf table in mahogany. Circa 1800-1810. The original is in the Metropolitan Museum of Art in New York.

Duncan Phyfe Flip Top table of mahogany, and an outstanding example of the type of work of this designer. The clustered lyre pedestal and the four curule legs always are identified with Phyfe.

*Mahogany stand Phyfe
design.*

*Turn top drop-leaf table, with lyre pedestal ends,
a characteristic Phyfe ornament.*

*Duncan Phyfe Sofa of carved mahogany showing
typical details of the style.*

a period of 52 years, but it was from 1795 to 1818 that his finest work appeared. This has been called the Adam-Sheraton period and represents the time during which Phyfe, because of his great love for classic line and proportion, went to these craftsmen for his inspiration.

Phyfe became an expert judge of mahogany. In handling this wood to obtain the best effects he never had a superior. At one time, so it is said, he paid as much as $1000 for a single log of Cuban mahogany. He had many wealthy patrons. It was at the suggestion of one of them that he changed his original name of Pyfe to Phyfe, early in his career.

Following the panic of 1818, which was an aftermath of the War of 1812, the Victorian influence began to creep in. Phyfe's work in this period showed steady deterioration. In spite of his great popularity and the classic lines of his really beautiful furniture he was not able to prevent the popular taste from going to the heavy designs in rosewood which he himself dubbed "butcher furniture". In attempting to keep pace with the popular taste he lost his individuality and artistry. For the genius of his youth, however, one can admire him and forgive the errors of his later life.

Phyfe Chair Slat

Phyfe's furniture was an elegant style. It possessed an effective lowness, together with excellent proportion and a highly developed purity of line. Phyfe was indeed a master of the curve.

His tables were usually supported at ends by coupled colonnettes or lyres. Supports for pedestals were frequently lyre-shaped also. Pedestals had three or four legs, and the curule was greatly favored. The straight-reeded legs which were used to some extent had simple turned feet.

Backs of chairs frequently showed the lyre motif, while the uprights sloped down and seemed to flow into the seat-rail. This was a very characteristic Phyfe detail. Other backs showed the X-shaped pieces straight or curved, with shaped horizontal bars between the uprights. Phyfe seldom used underbracing.

Phyfe Turning

The lyre was one of the most characteristic motifs used by this American designer. He was, however, fond of many classical motifs, such as drapery, swags, cornucopias crossed with a bow knot, trumpets, oval or rectangular medallions, rosettes; and such foliage motifs as the acanthus leaf, palm, oak, and laurel leaf. Wheat ears, crossed and tied with a bow knot, frequently were found; and the lion foot and the eagle wing were a part of the style. Carving, reeding and turning were important details, as were brass mounts. Veneering was used.

In recent years, there has been a revival in Duncan Phyfe furniture. Styles may come and go with the public's fancy, but such furniture as Phyfe's always will be beautiful. Not only is it on a classic foundation of correct proportion, but it is inseparably connected with the early history of this country. The furniture has a home-like appeal.

REPRODUCTIONS AND ADAPTATIONS

FOR thirty years the Century Furniture Company of Grand Rapids has devoted itself to faithful and accurate reproductions of traditional and historic furniture and the intelligent development of period adaptations.

By comparison, Century reproductions and the originals will be found to be identical in detail and in character, but far better in construction; and although made with no attempt at deception they are, nevertheless, frequently thought to be genuine antiques, and are often used in the finest homes to complete antique ensembles.

If the materials are available, a competent designer and skilled craftsman may make reproductions of original masterpieces with commendable fidelity, but to take from the works of the old masters only those elements one wishes to use; to preserve the high ideals of form and workmanship in all their inherent beauty and significance; to retain the subtle flavor of historic influences; and to weld to this venerable foundation the elements of modern research and utility—all these require a sense of discrimination, a combination of insight, ability and idealism that is indeed rare in an era of machine production and mass selling.

In this field Century—Grand Rapids excels. Furniture so designed is made of more than wood and fabric. It has a refining and cultural influence. It stimulates a desire for better living and becomes more valuable with use and with age.

In the factory showrooms of the Century Furniture Company in Grand Rapids, Century Productions in their entirety are on display throughout the year.

In New York at 227 E. 45th Street is located another showroom where a brilliant and comprehensive collection of Century Productions is on permanent display.

In Chicago at 161 E. Erie Street are the Century—Grand Rapids Showrooms where Century furniture may be seen.

The facilities of these showrooms include also competent decorative service in the correct furnishing of homes.

A visit will prove delightfully interesting and visitors are accorded every courtesy at our command.

CENTURY FURNITURE COMPANY
Grand Rapids, Michigan

A CHRONOLOGY
OF FURNITURE STYLES
IN
ENGLAND
FRANCE AND
AMERICA

ENGLAND

Sovereign	Date	Style	Principal Characteristics
Henry VII	1485-1509	*Gothic* Wood: Oak	Construction: straight line, massive. Trestle tables, stools, benches, chests.
Henry VIII	1509-1547	*Tudor* Wood: Oak	Construction: straight, massive and formal. Details: bulbous ornaments, Tudor rose, carving, linenfold, paneling. Renaissance motifs.
Elizabeth	1558-1603	*Tudor or Eliza-bethan* Wood: Oak	
James I	1603-1625	*Jacobean or Stuart*	Construction: straight, sturdy, squat. Draw-top, early gate-leg and refectory tables, wainscot chairs, cupboards.
Charles I	1625-1649	Wood: Oak	Details: twisted wood, paneling, carving, applied moldings and ornaments.
Cromwellian Era	1649-1660	*Commonwealth* Wood: Oak	Construction: straight. Chairs with low, square backs. Gate-leg tables and table chairs developed. Details: turning, paneling, carving.
Charles II	1660-1685	*Carolean, Stuart, or Restoration, Late Jacobean*	Construction: straight except for lavish use of Flemish scroll. Details: twist or spiral turning, cane backs and seats, carving, lacquer, marquetry, applied split balusters, upholstery, Spanish feet.
James II	1685-1688	Walnut replacing Oak	
William and Mary	1688-1702	*William and Mary* Wood: Walnut	Construction: curved line, lighter, graceful, adapted to human comfort. Details: serpentine stretchers, bun feet, cup turnings, hood tops, shaped aprons, paneling, marquetry.
Anne	1702-1714	*Queen Anne* Wood: Walnut Mahogany appears	Construction: curved line. Details: cabriole legs, club feet, solid splat, broken pediment, shell carvings.
George I-III	1714-1820	*Early Georgian* Wood: Walnut and Mahogany	Construction: similar to Queen Anne. Details: animal heads and paws, masks, swags, shells, scrolls, hoofs, lacquer, carving. *Style of Chippendale* Construction: curved and straight. Details: cabriole leg, claw and ball foot, pierced splat, ladder back. Chinese fret, carving of finest type. *Style of Hepplewhite* Construction: curved except chair legs. Details: shield and oval chair backs, square tapered legs, spade feet, serpentine fronts, painting, inlay, veneer. *Style of Adam Brothers* Construction: straight, small in scale. Details: legs square and tapered, or round and fluted. Oval and wheel backs, urn finials and other classic motifs, painting, inlay, carving. *Style of Sheraton* Construction: straight line. Details: chair backs square or oblong, legs tapered, square or round, turning, inlay, fluting, reeding.
		Georgian Wood: Mahogany and Satinwood	
George IV	1820-1830	*Empire* Wood: Mahogany	Construction: straight and curved. A debased form of French Empire.

FRANCE

Sovereign	Date	Style	Principal Characteristics
	12th, 13th and 14th Centuries	*Gothic* (originated in France)	Construction: straight, heavy, ecclesiastical type. Trestle, tables, stools, chests, cupboards, paneled back and canopy chairs.
Louis XII	1498-1515	Wood: Pine and Oak	Details: trefoil, quatrefoil, pointed arch, linenfold, panels, lion paws, heavy stretchers, elaborate carving.
Francis I	1515-1547	*Francois Premier* Wood: Oak (Renaissance in France)	Construction: straight, scale and less massive than Italian Renaissance.
Henry II	1547-1559	*Henri Deux*	Marked progress in wood carving, tapestry weaving, and manufacture of textiles.
Francis II	1559-1560		
Charles IX	1560-1574		
Henry III	1574-1589		
Henry IV	1589-1610	*Henri Quatre* Wood: Walnut	Decline of Renaissance. Furniture less refined and overloaded with meaningless ornament.
Louis XIII	1610-1643	*Louis Treize* Wood: Walnut	Construction: straight and curved. Details: scrolled or turned legs, spiral or twist turning, inlay, marquetry, upholstery becoming general.
Louis XIV	1643-1715	*Louis Quatorze* Wood: Oak Walnut Ebony	Construction: mainly straight, massive in scale, formal. High-backed, carved and upholstered chairs, commodes, and marble-topped console tables of special interest. Details: metal mounts, carving, painting, gilding, inlay, marquetry, lacquer, straight and curved stretchers, cloven hoofs.
The Regency	1715-1723	*Regence*	Transition from Louis Quatorze to Louis Quinze.
Louis XV	1715-1774	*Louis Quinze* Woods: Mahogany Walnut Ebony	Construction: curved line, elaborately decorated, expressing luxury, grace, and sensuous beauty. Details: cabriole leg with French scroll foot, bombe fronts, draped canopies over beds, rococo scroll, carving, inlay, marquetry, painting, gilding, veneering, metal mounts.
Louis XVI	1774-1793	*Louis Seize* Woods: Walnut Mahogany Satinwood	Construction: straight line, small in scale, classic in detail. Details: chair backs upholstered, carved or caned. Legs straight fluted or carved. Methods of decoration as in Louis XV period. Classical motifs including urns, pendant husks, lyres, oak leaves.
The Directory	1795-1799	*Directoire*	Transition from Louis XVI to Empire.
Napoleon	1799-1814	*Empire*	Construction: straight and curved. Proportions heavy, ponderous. Details: Paw and claw feet, columns, wings, cornucopias, pineapples, brass and ormolu mounts, painting, gilding.

AMERICA

Historical Events	Date	Style	Principal Characteristics
England lays claim to most of North America following visit of John Cabot	1497		
Jamestown Colony	1607	*Early American or Colonial*	Construction: straight, sturdy, in the Elizabethan and Jacobean traditions.
Landing of Pilgrims	1620	Woods: Oak Pine Maple Oak, Ash Hickory	Brewster and Carver chairs, the frames filled with spindles, also slat back chairs, from 1620. Trestle and gate-leg tables, chests carved and paneled, oak with pine lids. Court and press cupboards. 1640-1680.
Massachusetts Colony founded by Puritans	1630	Mahogany introduced 1710	Details: applied split spindles and bosses. Flemish paneling, carving, turning. Rush seats common. Charles II type of chair, high, narrow, backs and scrolled legs, 1666-1695. Apple or pear wood, usually painted.
Stamp Act	1765		Butterfly tables about 1670.
Battle of Bunker Hill	1775		Hadley chests carved and painted, produced in the Massachusetts Colony, 1690-1710. William and Mary and Queen Anne types introduced.
Declaration of Independence	1776	*Georgian Styles*	Secretaries, corner cupboards, Windsor and wing chairs, high boys, lowboys and dressers popular. Chippendale, Sheraton, Adam and Hepplewhite influence strongly evident in American products but the designs were simplified and inlay was usually replaced with carving.
Alliance with France	1778	Woods: Mahogany Cherry Walnut	Block front desks and secretaries, sideboards, piecrust tables.
Cornwallis' Surrender	1781	Curly Maple	Chest of drawers with serpentine fronts and bracket or ball and claw feet, 1760-1775. Sideboards about 1788.
Constitution of United States	1789	*American Empire*	Construction: curved and straight, massive and often clumsy. High and low four-posters with pineapple finials, sleigh beds, bureaus, chests, and sideboards, with fluted or twisted columns, lion paw feet, and swell fronts. Sofas with lion paw, eagle claw, or cornucopia supports and scrolled ends. Stencilled furniture about 1820.
War with England	1812	*Duncan Phyfe* 1795-1847 Wood: Mahogany	Details: as French Empire, carving taking place of metal mounts.

GLOSSARY

ACANTHUS LEAF A unit of classic decoration, adapted from the more or less ragged leaf of the acanthus plant, a native of Southern Europe. Use originated in antiquity; and the leaf is a distinguishing mark of the Corinthian capital.

ACORN TURNING A knob, pendant, or foot similar in shape to the acorn. Chiefly used during the Jacobean period.

ADELPHI Greek word meaning brothers. Adopted by the Brothers Adam, designers, as a trade mark.

ALMERY A type of cupboard, used as a receptacle for doles for pensioners or family retainers.

AMBOYNA A wood of peculiar grain, growing more beautiful with age. Used by Chippendale.

ANTHEMION Greek honeysuckle, conventionalized.

APRON A narrow strip of wood adjoining the base of cabinet bodies, seats, table tops, etc., extending between the tops of chairs or feet brackets.

ARABESQUE (in the Arabian style). Usually applied to designs composed chiefly of floriated scrolls. Introduced into English furniture in Tudor days.

ARCADE A series of arches, with columns or piers which support them.

ARMOIRE A large cupboard, for storing clothes. Probably an adaptation of the work aumbry, or ambry, used in early English times for the storing of arms and armor.

ARM SUPPORT The vertical or curved upright supporting the front end of chair arms.

ASTRAGAL A small convex beaded molding, usually placed at the junction of a pair of doors to exclude dust.

BALL FOOT A ball termination of a leg usually turned.

BALUSTER A small, slender turned column, usually swelled.

BANDING An inlay or marquetry device which gives a contrast in color or grain between the band and the surface it decorates.

BAROQUE (or Barocco). The Italian equivalent of the French rococo.

BEAD A small molding of nearly semi-circular section.

BERGERE A French arm chair.

BLOCK FOOT A square, vertical foot at the base of a straight, untapered leg.

BOMBE An outward swelling, curving or bulging.

BOSS A circular or oval protuberance for surface ornament.

BOULLE	Andre-Charles Boulle. A designer of the time of Louis XIV, noted for his exquisite marquetry, particularly the use of tortoise shell, veneer and metal inlays.
BOW TOP	A chair whose top rail is made of one low unbroken curve.
BUFFET	A small cupboard. Also a counter for refreshments. The French definition is: "a small sideboard, a place for the keeping of dishes."
BUN FOOT	A flattened ball or bun shape, with slender ankle above.
BUREAU	In France the bureau still is a desk, also the office where the desk is used. The word is from the Latin "burros", red, said to have been derived from a red cloth which covered a writing desk. America has adopted this furnishing with its convenient drawers for the bedroom, and retained the name.
CABOCHON	A plain round or oval surface, convex or concave, enclosed with ornamentation.
CABRIOLE	A term applied to legs that swell outward at the upper part or knee, and inward at the lower part or ankle. Employed with many variations and different feet.
CANAPE	A sofa or a divan. Originally a couch with mosquito curtains.
CARTOUCHE	A decorative device, originally based upon an unrolled scroll, the central surface often being used as a field for painted devices or inscriptions.
CARYATID	A conventionalized human figure serving as the top member of a pedestal or leg, and used as a support.
CERTOSINA	A variety of decoration, in which bone or ivory is inlaid into walnut, ebony, or another dark wood. Often highly geometrical.
COURT CUPBOARDS	Short cupboards. Originally small cupboards set on side tables, afterward combined into one piece.
CREDENCE	A forerunner of the modern sideboard. A term applied to antique pieces used for carving meats or displaying plate.
CROSS RAIL	A horizontal bar in a chair-back.
CYMA CURVE	A double or compounded "S" curve or wave.
DARBY & JOAN SETTEE	Small settee for two, the backs usually similar to two connected chair backs. Frequently called "love seats."
DENTILS	Rectangular blocks with spaces between, placed usually upon cornices.
DIAPER-WORK	A method of surface decoration consisting of a design of regular repeats.
DOLPHIN	A marine animal whose head and body, or head alone, is often used for conventionalized decorative purposes.

DROPPED SEAT	A concave seat, the middle and front of which are lower than the sides.
DUTCH FOOT	A simple pad frequently used as a terminal of cabriole legs.
EGG AND DART	A molding design of classic origin consisting of alternating eggs and darts.
ENDIVE	Water leaf, used in decorative effect.
ESCOLLOP SHELL	The Dutch cockle shell.
ESCRI-TOIRE	A writing desk with drawers and pigeon holes, frequently with secret compartments and treasure wells used for the safekeeping of various articles and papers. The word from which "secretary", (meaning secret) was derived.
ESCUT-CHEON	In heraldry, a shield with an armorial or heraldic device. Frequently these are carved upon furniture. Often the term applies, however, to a shaped plate or a brass fitting for a keyhole.
EVOLUTE	A recurrent wave motif for band or frieze decoration.
FARTHIN-GALE CHAIR	An armless upholstered chair of the early Stuart period, for the use of ladies wearing the enormous skirts of the time.
FAUTEUIL	An arm chair of French origin, open under the arms, in contradistinction to the bergere.
FIDDLE-BACK	A chair splat, the outlines of which somewhat resemble the shape of a violin.
FINIAL	A decorative finishing device for any sort of projecting upright.
FLEMISH SCROLL	A baroque form with the curve broken by an angle.
FLEUR-DE-LIS	A conventionalized flower used in decoration. A very old emblem. The Empress Theodora (A. D. 527) bore one in her crown. The coat of arms of ancient France (1179) was a blue field sprinkled with fleur-de-lis.
FLUTING	Channeling or grooving on a flat surface.
FLYING DISK	A flat disk centered between two outspread wings. A prominent motif in Egyptian decoration.
FOIL	A Gothic term for the intersecting point at the junctions of circular areas, as in trefoil, quatrefoil, cinquefoil.
FRET	Interlaced ornamental work sometimes perforated and sometimes applied on solid backgrounds.
GADROON	A carved moulding used chiefly upon table tops and chair edges.
GESSO	A plastic substance originally made of plaster and sugar, molded into decorative shapes, in a bas-relief and allowed to harden, then pointed or gilded.

GLASTON-BURY CHAIR	An X-framed ecclesiastical Gothic seat with sloping panelled back. Its arms had a drooping curve in which a priest's vestments rested.
GOBELIN	A tapestry factory in France which developed rare art under Louis XIV.
GRIFFIN	A chimerical beast employed in decoration in the early Georgian designs.
GROS POINT	A type of embroidery.
GUILLOCHE	An ornamental pattern of two or more interlacing bands or ribbons. The intertwined sections frequently enclosing rosettes or other details.
HIGHBOY	A tall chest of drawers.
HOOD	A shaped top to cabinet work.
HUSKS	A form of ornamentation of foliage or flowers usually used in pendant manner.
INTARSIA	See Marquetry.
INVERTED CUP	A turning found particularly in William and Mary furniture which has the appearance of a cup up-side-down.
KNEE	The uppermost part of cabriole leg.
LADDER-BACK	A chair-back in which a series of horizontal cross rails are used instead of a splat, giving the effect of a ladder.
LAURELLING	The laurel leaf motif.
LINEN FOLD	A carved or painted pattern of ecclesiastical origin and late Gothic period. Resembling a scroll of linen, it is emblematic of the cloth placed over the consecrated bread at communion.
LOTUS	The Egyptian water lily, conventionalized forms of which are found in classic ornamentation.
LOZENGE	A diamond shaped decorative motif.
LUNETTE	A half moon shaped ornament.
LYRE	A decorative motif selected from the musical instrument of the same name.
MARQUETRY	Flat, colored decorations formed by patterns of various woods, tortoise shell, bone, ivory or metals, inlaid into a panel or surface. In "Intarsia" the design is sunk into the solid wood. In "Marquetry" the design is often fitted to corresponding holes in a thin wood veneer, which is then glued to the furniture.
MASQUE	A human, animal, or a grotesque face without the rest of the body. Used as an ornament.
MOTIF	The guiding or controlling idea manifested in a work or any part of a work. The dominant feature.

MULLION	A slender strip of wood separating the various panes in a window or door.
OGEE	A form composed of two opposite cyma curves with their convex sides meeting in a point.
ORMOLU	A metal resembling gold, used for elaborate metal mounts.
PATERA	A small disk, oval or round, used as a base for ornamental detail. The "paterae" were plate-like vessels used for the Roman sacrifices to the gods. Introduced as an ornament upon friezes and later adopted in decorating furniture.
PATINA	A soft surface film upon a wooden or metallic surface, caused by exposure, age, use, or the action of chemical fumes.
PEDIMENT	A molded or otherwise ornamented structure placed above a cornice. The classic pediment was of simple triangular shape, but it since has been variously developed. It is said to be "broken" when the lines of its sides fail to join.
PENDANT	A hanging ornament.
PETIT POINT	A kind of embroidery.
PIE-CRUST TABLE	A smaller center table, the edges of which are scalloped and slightly raised.
PIER TABLE	A table similar to a console table used under a hanging mirror.
PILASTER	A flat column attached to the face of a plain surface, mainly as an ornamental support for an arch, cornice, or other superstructure.
PRIE-DIEU CHAIR	A high backed chair, with a narrow shelf, rail, or pad upon which the user may rest his arms while kneeling in the seat.
PRINCE OF WALES FEATHERS	Three decorative feathers somewhat in the shape of the conventional fleur-de-lis. Used largely by Hepplewhite. The motto of the prince, "Ich dien", meaning, "I serve", also was employed occasionally.
QUATREFOIL	A conventionalized adaptation of the four-leaf clover.
RINCEAU	A classic ornamental device, favored by the Brothers Adam, composed of intertwining stalks of acanthus or other foliage.
REEDING	A series of parallel lines of small convex or beaded mounting, raised from the surface. The reverse of fluting which is sunk or grooved.
REFECTORY TABLE	A long, narrow dining table of early origin. Later they were smaller but were extended by means of an ingenious under-leaf at each end.
RIBBAND-BACK	A chair back with a ribbon motif ornament.

ROCOCO — An elaborate form of ornamentation full of curves, rocks, and shells and other conventionalized rustic detail, compounded from the words "rocaille" (rock work) and "coquille" meaning shell.

ROMAYNE — A type of ornamentation employing human heads upon medallions.   Early Tudor adaptations of Renaissance details.

SALTIRE — A straight X-shaped stretcher.

SCAMNUM — A Roman bench.

SEIGNEUR-IAL CHAIR — A stately high-backed seat for the master.   The lower part frequently composed a locker.

SERPENTINE FRONT — A front shaped with a waving or serpentine curve.

SHIELD — The conventional shield shape used for chair-backs and mirrors.

SKIRT — Apron.

SPINDLE — A slender turned vertical baluster.

SPIRAL TURNING — A twisted form of turning.

SPLAT — A central member of a chair-back.

SPOONING — A chair-back shaped to fit the contour of the human body.

SQUAB — A loose cushion.

STRAP WORK — An ornament consisting of narrow bands crossed or interlaced in various patterns.

STRETCHER — The underbracing of chairs, tables and other furniture, originally serving also as a foot rest.

SWAG — A festoon of draperies, leaves, or flowers.

TESTER — The upper or canopy part of a high poster bedstead.

TOP RAIL — The top member of a chair-back.

TUDOR ROSE — A decorative motif taken from the emblems used by the House of York (White rose) and the House of Lancaster (Red rose) who fought for the English throne in the 15th Century, in what was known as the War of Roses.

TURKEY WORK — A form of embroidery used in the 18th Century, the name being a vulgarization of the word "Turkish."

UPRIGHT — An extension of back legs supporting the chair-back.

VENEER — A thin coating of ornamental wood permitting a display of figured grain not possible otherwise. This is glued to the body of plain solid wood. The idea that veneered furniture is cheapened furniture has long since passed as an erroneous idea. Veneered furniture today represents the highest attainment of the furniture maker's art.